FACEBOOK MARKETING

World-Class Techniques for Optimizing Your Page, Increasing Likes, and Creating Captivating Facebook Ads That Produce Powerful Results (2022 Guide for Beginners)

Fred Hart

TABLE OF CONTENTS

INTRODUCTION

Facebook connects people who choose to make information about their activities and hobbies available by using the like button or sharing content with their friends. Its success stems from the ability of users to form networks with their friends, relatives, or acquaintances and connect with them at any time of day.

The social network's role can also be conceived as a place where you can find customers for your online commercial reality, as well as a platform where you can exchange photos, videos, and thoughts about your personal world; with some precautions, you can take advantage of the commercial functionality.

By connecting the firm and potential customers' contacts, it is possible to speak directly, even in a pleasant manner, developing a genuine tie of trust between merchant and buyer, expanding the reputation of your brand, and making yourself known to new users.

Facebook is the most popular social network in the world, and it has become one of the most frequented websites in history, with over a billion visitors.

There are 1.32 billion active users worldwide. This solution allows you to reach your target customers in a timely and targeted manner.

Facebook is a very powerful communication platform for businesses, as well as an effective tool for advertising your company and attracting new clients. The following are some of the reasons why you should use it:

You may identify your consumers' target demographics by using filters such as age, interests, and geography.

Many of your consumers have a Facebook page that you can contact.

You can broaden your network of connections associated with your firm.

Facebook can assist you in establishing trust with your customers.

Through their interactions with your posts, you may gauge your consumers' contentment with your products and services.

It enables you to understand how competitors in your industry move by reading their papers.

Increase your company's global awareness, not just locally.

FACEBOOK

CHAPTER 1
SIGN UP FOR FACEBOOK

This chapter explains how to start and open a new Facebook account, as well as how to create a profile and add friends.

Facebook

Even though the success of social media has been disruptive and involves entire generations, there are still many people who do not know what Facebook is or do not understand what it is, who see this website as more of a toy for children, a "Big Brother" site where everyone can be observed, or simply a waste of time. Although these issues can be shared in certain ways, it all depends on how you use Facebook.

In this chapter, we'll show you how to join Facebook and join over a billion already registered and active members in the web's largest community, so you can build a new profile and start adding friends, relatives, childhood friends, or acquaintances.

How to Sign Up for Facebook

Although it is not a complicated operation in and of itself, it is always a good idea to review the technique to sign up for Facebook, because a rookie user or someone who is new to technology may be confused or unable to submit the correct information.

Sign up for Facebook

Simply access the Facebook.com website to log in and register.

Let us not forget that Facebook is completely free and does not charge any fees.

Using a fictitious name on Facebook can just help to build a parallel virtual life that is diametrically opposed to the real one. This is by no means the intention of this social network, which was designed to connect genuine people, therefore anyone who signed up with fictitious or contrived names would be better off using other similar sites like Twitter. Even the date of birth must be entered correctly in order to use Facebook services based on this day, such as horoscopes and birthday reports.

On the home screen, click the green "Create account" button, and then enter your true name and surname, email address or mobile number (real and to be confirmed), date of birth, and gender (male, female, or other). After clicking the "Signup" button, you will receive an email to the email address you provided or an SMS to the phone number you provided with a link to click or a code to input to validate your identity.

Following confirmation of the email address or cellphone number, Facebook recommends searching for friends using the email address. This will be the most amusing part, but it is actually the last thing you should do when making an account. In fact, sending friend invitations is pointless if the profile is white and empty, with no information that may be used to identify the person. Because there are many homonyms and false profiles on Facebook, it is difficult to get approved as a friend if your profile is incomplete.

Facebook will then ask you to fill out your profile information. I recommend you skip this step as well, at least for the time being.

Personalize Your Facebook Account

We can now begin constructing your Facebook account by uploading a photograph of yourself. The term "Facebook" is a combination of the terms "Face" and "Book" and is so named for a reason: it is necessary for everyone to have a profile photo of themselves in order to be recognized before adding friends. Approximately 95% of members have a profile picture. We recommend using your own pictures, not the dog's or someone else's because Facebook is pointless and dull if you are unrecognizable.

Furthermore, after uploading your profile picture from your computer, you enable the Photo tab, from which you can build photo albums.

Please keep in mind that the profile photo, as well as the optional cover photo, are always available to everyone.

Change the privacy settings as needed.

This is the most difficult aspect of Facebook since there are so many options and settings to adjust in order to determine how you want to be seen by others and how you want to be searched and found. To configure privacy, access the "Privacy Control" menu by pressing the arrowhead in the upper right, then "Settings" and "Privacy."

We click on each box and change the settings as needed, configuring the most sensitive information to be exposed only to friends (or only to ourselves) and configuring the information we want to be visible to many more people like Friends of friends.

If we want to meet a large number of individuals, we must make some settings "Public," so that all Facebook users can read them. We can also choose who reads the things we publish. We recommend that you set "Friends" for personal postings and "Public" for those that we wish to support or that everyone can view.

Fill up your profile information

Now is the moment to complete your profile information. Click the Info tab on the main profile page, then Edit and fill up the blanks with information about your present and former lives. Alternatively, you may fill out the various sections of the profile by clicking here.

You shouldn't be scared to write true information about

yourself if your privacy settings have been appropriately established because they will only be available to whoever you choose. The section on "Education and work" allows you to reconnect with former school classmates and coworkers, while "Interests and preferences" can help you meet new individuals who share your interests while you're out and about (personally I have not written anything here).

Create a username

One item that many Facebook users, both new and old, frequently overlook is the ability to modify their profile address. We can find the username by going to "Settings" -> "General." This name converts your profile's internet address, or URL, to something like www.facebook.com/pomhey. My advice is to use the true name, possibly in conjunction with the formula name. surname. Facebook profiles have virtually become online identity cards, and each user's name has almost become a trademark, unique and unreplicable by anyone.

Make New Friends

After almost entirely filling out the profile and correctly configuring the privacy settings, it's time to use the social network for its intended purpose: to find and add friends.

It is possible that, during the first setup, Facebook will propose certain people to add as friends by filling out various fields connected to school and employment. Friends can be found using the Facebook Home search field, although it is best to do this first, especially if you have just signed up, and leave Facebook to the chore of issuing friend requests based on your e-mail provider's address book.

Facebook is authorized to access the online address books of Gmail, Yahoo mail, Skype, and many more online services through the "Find friends" tab.

Make a list of buddies.

The final thing you should do on Facebook is building friend lists. Because we may have hundreds or thousands of contacts on Facebook, it is best to organize them into lists so that, in the privacy settings, you can decide who to show what and who will be able to read all the posts we publish, excluding in the case of some group of acquaintances, people added without criteria, or relatives (who will be able to read only what we want to show).

Now, the Facebook experience should be easy, enjoyable, and, why not, productive. You can install the software (while keeping an eye out for potential viruses), send private messages, create new friends, meet new people, chat, and so on.

CHAPTER 2
ACCESS AND POST

This chapter contains a list of 12 key rules for using Facebook that may be useful for individuals who are just getting started, newbies, or those who wish to explore every facet of the social network.

1) How to Begin with Facebook

Although it may appear unusual, we can still encounter people who haven't joined Facebook or who have only recently begun to be so technologically savvy. This tutorial may be worthless for many people, but because so many people still use Facebook as if it were a foreign tool, it is necessary to instantly understand all the tricks of the trade so that you are not caught off guard and can utilize the blue network like true professionals.

In this chapter, we will thus describe and explain the essential elements of Facebook for beginners and those who find it difficult to locate the different options, so that we may customize the social network to our needs and avoid undesirable situations dictated by inexperience.

We see the principles of Facebook, its primary features, policies, and restrictions, point by point, just like in a refresher course. Even the most seasoned users, when viewed through the eyes of a newcomer, will be able to express their thoughts on the world's most popular social network.

First and foremost, I recommend reading the guide on how to join Facebook, establish a new account, and create a profile. We may begin exploring all of the features immediately after signing up and creating a basic profile.

2) Timeline on Facebook (or personal page)

Before you start looking for friends, you should finish the timeline, which is your own profile page. You must add a profile photo and a large cover photo, as well as an explanation of your job history and relationships, to the timeline. This final point could be optional.

It is termed a timeline because it is feasible to incorporate the information, major goals achieved, and memories spanning a lifetime on the page. We can read the guide to the settings and visibility of the new timeline profile to learn how to use it. You can utilize various ideas and web programs to make the cover of your Facebook page.

3) Friends

Start the search and add some buddies when you've completed a section of the journal.

Because many of your colleagues, family members, schoolmates, and neighbors are likely to be registered, looking for them will be a breeze owing to the automatic function of friend referrals.

Many people do not want to be seen by old friends or colleagues, but I strongly encourage them not to be shy or afraid of anything because you can add a person without ever communicating with him/her (if you don't want to).

4) News

Finding Facebook friends is vital not just for connecting with them, but also for staying up to date on their latest news, views, and activities. To get this information, go to the News area and read the news, which is organized by chronology and popularity.

Everything is in the news section: friends' status updates, fresh images, links to articles, and so on.

One of Facebook's most recent adjustments was to sort news through an algorithm that determines which ones should be ranked first.

If you prefer to see things in chronological order, go to the top of the page and pick Most Recent instead of Top News.

5) The status report

A status update is a message that is shared in your diary and is available to friends, either some of them or all of them openly, depending on your choices.

You can convey your current activity or where you are (via a "check-in") in a status update, or you can post a link to an interesting article or site, share images and videos, and even construct a survey.

You can create a status update from the news section or the timeline's top. Because Facebook is now a place for sharing good information with the goal of fostering conversation, it's not worth writing foolish or worthless facts.

6) Facebook Live Stories

Instead of Facebook status updates, we can build tales similar to Instagram.

The stories can also be published from a PC and allow you to share photos, short videos, or personal messages with effects or images from the Internet; the most interesting feature is that the stories on Facebook will be deleted forever after 24 hours, so the messages left on the story must be short, impactful, but without the need to keep them. Something geared for young people, but valuable to discover and use.

7) Brands, organizations, and businesses

While friends are an important component of Facebook, they aren't the only people with whom you can communicate. Brands are represented by pages that represent organizations, companies, fan groups, locations, or other entities rather than persons.

Companies such as Coca-Cola and Disney, as well as small businesses, utilize Facebook to engage, share, and solicit feedback from customers and fans. Following the pages might be useful for receiving company updates and promotions.

8) Clicking the "Like" button

The "Like" button, which can be seen on practically every website, is one of Facebook's most powerful and important tools.

It conveys to friends your admiration or support for the activities, brands, and articles you've read.

The "Like" button can be found on Facebook for practically any sort of material, including status updates, images, comments, pages, applications, and adverts. When you "Like" something outside of Facebook.com, it appears in your timeline, where friends can remark on the action. Keep in mind, however, that Facebook tracks activity and "Likes" in order to "better the quality" of adverts on the site, and that Facebook may share this behavioral data with third parties (anonymously).

9) The labels

Tags on Facebook let you reference another Facebook user in a photo, a status update, a narrative, or a comment.

When you tag someone in a photo, the individual is notified, and the marked photo appears on their timeline (assuming they haven't turned off the tagging feature). The tag tool promotes conversation and establishes new connections between people.

It is crucial to remember that everyone has different tagging preferences: some individuals can immediately check the material in which they have been tagged and then remove them by rejecting the quote, possibly because they do not like the photo or do not want to be visible in that photo. The "Privacy" settings area contains tag settings and management.

10) Privacy

You could write an entire book about Facebook privacy, but in this case, I'll be brief.

On Facebook, we can create a special list of friends who will not be able to read all that has been published in my journal. The public profile, which is visible to everyone, friends, and strangers alike, can be scrutinized in every way. Almost all profile sections include an edit button that allows you to control who can see the information you've posted.

Simply go to "Settings -> Privacy" and act as we feel most appropriate to thoroughly verify the privacy settings.

11) Subscribe to and follow updates from people you don't know.

We can enable the Follow function on some profiles, company pages, and public celebrity profiles.

Following celebrities, journalists, and other prominent figures who want to communicate with fans without giving them access to their private profiles would find this option especially beneficial. Those who subscribe to my updates will be able to see everything I put in the diary with the "Public" setting.

12) Facebook for mobile devices

Facebook has an app for Android smartphones and tablets, as well as an app for iPhone/iPad that works so well that it can replace access to Facebook from a PC (practically all users use the app instead of the site).

With Facebook, it is possible to share one's location at any time, telling where you are, in which street, square, club, or restaurant, and also to search for individuals, friends, or otherwise, in the vicinity, using a mobile phone.

CHAPTER 3

MANAGING A FACEBOOK PAGE

To properly administrate a co page, you must be active and show consistent dedication. Fortunately, Facebook provides a plethora of tools to assist you in managing pages effectively.

Go to a Facebook page. Launch Facebook. Using a browser, go to https://www.facebook.com/. If you are already logged in, you will be taken to the main Facebook page.

If you are not already logged in, enter your e-mail address and password in the upper right corner, then click "Log in."

Select "Manage Pages." This option is available from the drop-down menu. A list of all the pages you manage will be displayed. You'll also notice a small summary of some of the pages you manage at the top of the drop-down menu.

Choose a page. To open the page you want to manage, click on its name. At that moment, you can begin performing all of the necessary operations.

Making a Post on a Page

Click in the text box labeled "Write a post..." It can be found at the top of the page. This section will be chosen and you will be able to write a post in it.

The textual portion of the post is referred to as "copy." Copies for business pages should be brief and only a few lines long. The tone should be straightforward and informal. Make an effort to be nice and enthusiastic.

You may also see individual post kinds by clicking on the question mark icon situated below the "Write a post..." text box (such as surveys or job postings).

If necessary, provide an image with your post. While photographs are optional, they give a personal touch to posts and make them more intriguing. To upload a photo, click "Photo/video" in the "Write a post..." box, then "Upload photo/video" and choose a photo or video from your computer.

Click the blue "Share now" button placed underneath the text box.

The content will be published on your page right away.

The "Publish" button appears at the bottom of the post on some pages.

To get the most out of the page, publish frequently but not excessively. If you make too many posts, your page may be marked as spam.

Post during peak hours (between 6 p.m. and 11 p.m.) to get more responses.

Make a post-appointment. After composing a post, perform the following to schedule its publishing on a specified day or time:

Under the "News section" title, click the "Share now" option (do not click on the blue button at the bottom of the post). If the "Post" button shows at the bottom of the post, click on the down arrow to its right

pick "Schedule" from the drop-down menu

enter a day and time, and then click on "Program."

Message Reading and Replying

Select Mail. It's near the top of the screen, close to the "Page" tab, and just below the search bar. In this section, you can review the communications you've received.

If you are opening your email for the first time, you may be prompted to click "Get Started."

Select a conversation. In the left side panel, the talks are listed. Conversations that are new or contain fresh messages are highlighted in red.

If you have a large number of discussions, you can use the search bar at the top of the list to find a specific one. Click in the text box labeled "Write a response..." It's at the very bottom of the dialogue you initiated.

Enter your response. Enter your response by typing it in and pressing "Enter."

The message will be delivered.

Messages cannot be sent through a corporate page. Only communications sent to you by other users can be replied to.

Change between inboxes. Messenger, Facebook, and Instagram notifications all have their own inboxes. You can switch between boxes by clicking on the Messenger, Facebook, or Instagram logos in the top left corner, accordingly.

The Facebook tab displays the comments, reactions, and reviews posted on your page, whilst the Instagram tab displays the comments left under Instagram photos.

If you have not linked your Instagram account to your Facebook account, you will not be able to see the messages you have received on this social network in the Instagram tab.

Messages can be turned off as necessary. If you don't want visitors to text your page, do the following:

click on "Settings" in the upper right corner;

click on "General" on the left side of the page;

click on "Messages";

remove the check mark from the box "Allow people to

contact my page privately by showing the message button";

click on "Save changes".

Observing Alerts and Insights

Select Notifications. It's located near the top of the page, next to the "Mail" tab. Filter notifications by clicking on "Like," "Comments," or "Shares" in the left-hand column.

Examine your alerts. Scroll through the list of page-related notifications.

To view a notification, choose it. When you click on notice, it will open in the context in which it is positioned. For example, if you received a notification because someone made a remark under a post, clicking on the notification will open that post and display the relevant comment.

Select the Insights tab. It can be found at the top of the page. It displays a number of choices for monitoring page traffic and general performance.

Examine the page's statistics. Choose a category, then read the information on the page that appears. In this manner, you can utilize the data from the "Insights" area to determine which actions are effective and which need to be tweaked slightly.

Modifying the Page Settings

Select "Settings." This button is positioned in the upper right corner, just below the Facebook notification indicator.

Choose a category. Click on one of the following categories on the left side of the page:

General: This category focuses on the most common page settings, such as age limits.

Messages: This category contains options related to email and page messages.

Templates and tabs: this option allows you to adjust the properties related to the page's structure and appearance.

Posting attribution: In this section, you may choose whether postings are automatically credited to your primary Facebook page or account.

Notifications: In this section, you may modify the settings that define which activities create notifications and on which platforms you will get them.

Messenger platform: this option allows you to customize how the website appears on Messenger.

Videos: this section contains the settings for the videos on the page.

Page roles: You can assign a specific role to each page administrator in this area.

People and other pages: This section displays a list of people and other pages who have expressed an interest in yours.

Permissions: In this section, you can connect your Facebook Ads account to the page.

Branded content: this area deals with branded post settings and allows you to decide which partner pages can tag you in posts.

Instagram: This section contains settings for your Instagram account and allows you to link it to the page if you haven't previously.

Highlighted: This option provides a list of pages that you have liked and highlighted on your own.

Cross-posting: This option allows you to add one or more pages to which you can repost the same content that you have published on your own.

Choose a sub-category. Each category in the settings offers a list of options that can be adjusted. These options differ depending on the category chosen. In the center of the page, click on the option you want to edit.

Change the settings to meet your requirements. This, too, differs depending on the category.

Changes should be saved. Click "Save" or "Save changes" if prompted. The page should reload and display the options you've chosen. Not all options necessitate that you save your modifications.

Using a Mobile Phone to Manage a Facebook Page

Launch Facebook. Tap the app icon, which is a white "f" on a dark blue backdrop. The "News section" of your logged-in account will be displayed.

If you haven't already, enter your email address and/or password when prompted.

Navigate to the page. Tap the bottom or top right corner. Tap "Pages" in the resulting menu, followed by the page name. The option "Pages" is located next to an orange flag icon.

Make a post. Press "Publish" at the top of the page, then input the post you wish to publish and tap "Publish" or "Next" at the top right.

Then, choose a publication option and choose "Share now" or "Share."

To add a photo to the post, hit "Photos/Videos" below and then choose an image (or movie) from your smartphone's camera roll. Make a post-appointment. After you've finished writing the post and clicked "Share" or "Next," you can schedule it for a different day and/or time by completing the following:

tap "Now" to the right of the "Share" title (on Android, tap

"Publish Now" at the top of the menu);

tap "Schedule";

select a date and time;

tap "Done" (iPhone) or "Set date" (Android).

Examine the page notifications. Tap the "Activities" tab at the top of the screen (below the search bar), then select "Notifications" from the drop-down menu that displays. The page alerts are displayed in this area. When you tap on a notification, it will open in the context it is now in. If you receive a notification about a post, for example, touching it will open the post in question.

Examine the messages on the page. If you wish to see them, quit the notifications page by tapping the "Back" button, then hit the "Messages" item in the menu.

Messages can be accessed from the page by tapping "Activities" at the top of the screen, followed by "Messages."

Modify the page settings. To access the settings, go to the "Page" tab and then tap "Edit page" under the cover photo. In the resulting menu, select "Change settings." You will be able to choose a category, a configuration, and the necessary changes.

The "General Settings" category is the most often utilized.

CHAPTER 4

12 HIDDEN FUNCTIONS TO USE FACEBOOK AS EXPERTS DO

This chapter offers 12 expert-recommended strategies for using the Facebook timeline, including the most helpful and hidden features. Facebook is a constantly evolving world that evolves over time, sometimes with less noticeable and more subtle modifications.

To summarize what is now the world's most populous social

network, let's look at the 12 most useful but also somewhat hidden capabilities of Facebook.

These are 12 Facebook tips that only the most knowledgeable users are aware of, but that everyone should be aware of in order to improve the timeline, optimize what shows on the home and timeline, and better control the applications.

1) View photographs in full-screen mode.

The Facebook photo viewer has gone through various iterations, from a fixed page with comments at the bottom to a pop-up with a black background and comments on the side.

As a result, it is able to view images from a Facebook album in full-screen mode.

Click on an image in an album and hover over it until a menu appears at the bottom of the image.

Select "Options" and then "View fullscreen."

To return to regular mode, hit the Esc key or the "X" in the upper right corner.

2) Disable programs

The new Facebook apps interact with the timeline by sharing information about what was done or read.

You must change some settings if you do not want your activity to be shared on social media platforms.

Enter the "Account settings" menu by clicking the down arrow at the upper right.

Go to the "Applications" tab and select "Edit," then select the apps you want to keep private by selecting the "Only Me" option.

This option can be altered each time an application is installed.

3) Make a list depending on your interests.

Facebook's news "lists" are a new feature that allows you to categorize content from specific pages or persons by topic. If you follow updates from blogs or cooks, technological news, current events, and so on, you may then develop a recipe list.

4) Perform a Facebook search.

The regular Facebook search does not operate well unless the language is set to English.

In this instance, a whole new universe of possibilities opens up, and it is truly possible to learn everything there is to know about a person and his or her relationships with others.

5) Rearrange the photographs on your Facebook timeline.

When you publish a photo on Facebook, it is shown in the timeline in the center.

You can select which area of the image to preview if the image is large.

Choose the "Reposition photo" function by clicking on the pencil at the top right ("edit or remove" button) of the photo to be rearranged that shows in the journal.

Drag the image left or right with the mouse to find the optimal position.

6) Hide from chat pals.

On Facebook chat, you can go offline for everyone or conceal simply for certain friends with whom you do not wish to communicate.

You can prevent being phoned by going offline.

To do so, click on the person's name in the chat column on the right as if you were starting a conversation.

Click the gear icon in the communication window, then pick "Go offline for [Name]."

7) Review and approve tags

Before being published, each tag placed by a friend on a photo or in a post must be approved by the individual listed.

However, this only happens if this person's tag control is turned on.

Click on "Change options" in the "Timeline and adding tags" area of the "Privacy settings" drop-down menu at the top right of the Facebook page.

If you enable the option "Check the posts in which your friends have tagged you," you will be required to accept every tag placed by friends and non-friends alike.

8) Remove unwelcome content from the front page.

To some extent, you can manage what shows in your Facebook news feed.

Change the settings by clicking on the pencil symbol that shows when you hover over the "News" item in the left column on the site.

It is possible to hide select people's messages from the core news stream, as well as specific programs and page updates, from the small window.

9) Form a secret society.

It is possible to set up a private Facebook group that only the founder and his friends have access to.

The hidden group is a fun method to create a private forum, a club where you can discuss information with a small group of people.

To begin the secret group, go to the "Groups" section in the left column of the main page and select "Create Group."

After naming the group, select the icon from the drop-down menu, invite friends, and then choose the "secret" option.

10) Include high-quality photos.

When you post a photo to Facebook, it is resized and not in high resolution by default.

If you wish to publish your images in the highest possible quality, you must first create a new album, upload the photos, and then select the "High Quality" option from the drop-down menu.

11) Disappear from Facebook for a short period of time

It is possible to deactivate Facebook and vanish as if the account and profile never existed in order to temporarily halt all actions.

Simply logging back into your account will restore everything and allow you to resume where you left off.

12) Eye-catching postings

If you read colored posts with large writings on Facebook at home, those are generated by the Facebook app on your mobile device.

CHAPTER 5

34 TRICKS FOR ADDING FUNCTIONS

This chapter concentrates on the best Facebook tactics, including more than 20 hidden pages, secret settings, and special functionalities for taking full advantage of the social network's capabilities.

Facebook is today's leading digital square, a place where we can all exchange our thoughts, opinions, and comments about anything. However, this social network has grown rapidly over the years, with over a billion users and a plethora of frequently hidden capabilities that are difficult to encompass in a single essay.

Most of these Facebook methods have previously been investigated in other publications, so in this chapter, we offer a great review with the finest, which primarily discusses hidden pages, secret options to edit, and little-known ways to customize the profile to the best. and the flow of information

Read hidden messages received on Facebook

Most people do not know that not only those received from friends are collected in the message box, but also those received from non-friends, for which there is no notification, and which remain hidden. It is therefore worthwhile if it has never been done before, to take a look at these messages to see if we have been joined by some old friends or if there is something interesting or funny.

Then open the messages page on the Facebook site and click, at the top left, on "Message requests" and on "More> With filters".

Check active connections to Facebook

From the account settings, in the "Security" section, you can check the "devices from which you are logged in" to be able to check if someone is using our account and, possibly, to close the connection from other computers that may be used.

From the same settings section, you can also check where and how we connected to Facebook.

See hidden Facebook photos of people you don't have among your friends

With a fantastic trick, it is possible to see the hidden photos on Facebook of everyone, even non-friends, which are collected on a special hidden page.

See contacts and numbers shared on Facebook, even of people who are not Facebook members

On a special page, you can see all the numbers that the Facebook Messenger app installed on the mobile has extracted from the phone book in an attempt to find registered friends. These numbers are collected on a private page and can be erased forever.

Use secret emojis

You can leave comments with the classic Moji or the secret ones.

Transfer files with Facebook

Not everyone knows that Facebook allows you to exchange

files with friends through its chat, albeit with some limitations.

See news from our best friends first

While the news flow of the news page on Facebook is controlled by an algorithm, it is still possible to customize how these are sorted by specifying which friends and which pages are most important to us, whose posts we want to appear before those are published by others.

Also, it's worth cleaning up Facebook by hiding news from boring sites, groups, apps, pages, and friends.

Find out how Facebook knows all our preferences

This is a special private page where you can check how Facebook sees us, that is what we like, and the profile that appears to advertisers.

It is also possible to prevent Facebook from seeing the history of the sites visited.

Change profile picture in a special way

For the profile photo, Facebook has added some possibilities to make yourself more original, and, in particular, it allows you to set a temporary profile photo and use a video instead of the profile picture.

Use Facebook as a blog

If you want to write long posts and keep them organized so you can find them easily as you would with a blog, you can use the not too well-known "Facebook Notes" feature.

Save news and links on Facebook

Every time you come across something interesting you can put the "like", but if you want to keep a link or a post that you want to read calmly or that you want to keep, you can save it with the special, a little hidden, save button.

See details for each friendship

For each friend, there is a special page that shows us what we have in common: friends, photos, posts, places visited, and other things.

PC chat tricks

Among the best tricks for Facebook chat, if used from a PC, there is the one to disable the read confirmation of messages to hide "Read" and "Is typing…" in Facebook chat.

Furthermore, even without using extensions, it is possible to hide in order not to be seen online by some users or to remain invisible to everyone

Invite friends to an event

You can invite all your friends to an event or become a fan of a Facebook page using two special extensions from the Chrome and Firefox browsers that enable a button to select all in one click. For Chrome, the extension is "Invite All Friends".

Program the status update on Facebook

Programming the status update on Facebook in a postdated way means setting the status and saying that you want to publish it in the future, in a few hours or in a few days.

This can be useful if you want to appear active when in reality you have been offline for some time and then you can schedule the status update on Facebook for every day that you are not planning to use Facebook. It might be helpful, now that I think about it, to update your status to look sick at home while on vacation.

Facebook backup

To back up the contact list and save their names and email addresses and to save private messages on the computer, there is the function to download messages, address book, and data from Facebook.

Temporarily suspend the profile

If you are tired of being on Facebook but don't want to lose everything and want to keep the possibility of being able to return to it in the future, you can simply deactivate your Facebook account temporarily.

Alternatively, you can also hide your Facebook profile and make yourself invisible.

Can a Facebook account be hacked?

If there was an easy trick for this, it would be a bane for our favorite social network. However, a lot of guides have already been written about techniques for stealing a Facebook account.

Search on Facebook

Facebook's default search engine is very limited and hardly works for anything other than finding people.

However, if you activate the American version of Facebook, then you can take advantage of that search engine that has never been released for legal privacy reasons.

Conversely, you can also use Facebook without being found or searched for.

Upload photos to Facebook at maximum quality

When you upload photos to Facebook, the site compresses them by default.

However, there is an option to upload the photos at maximum quality, in order to avoid them being compressed, to make them look more beautiful.

Facebook to find shops or to buy things

To expand its business, Facebook is gearing up to challenge online shopping giants like eBay.

Specifically, Facebook groups can be used to buy and sell, and it is possible to search for shops and businesses on a Facebook map.

Add a fixed message and featured photo to your Facebook profile

This is a trick that has been active for about a year, which still few people know, which allows you to create a mini-biography and show a permanent photo under the main one of the profile.

Receive notifications from the Facebook site such as the app This trick is especially useful if you are using the Facebook site

on your mobile instead of the application.

Secret words with animations: kisses, balloons, thumbs

Leave all Facebook groups and pages together at once

Delete all posts and Facebook "Likes" in one click

Write lists as statuses on Facebook

Add a song to listen to on the profile

Lists of interest

Creating lists of interest on Facebook allows you to create special sections in the home to find updates of pages followed or people who have something in common. For example, you can create an interest list for technology news and include sites and blogs.

Couple page

If you have set up a romantic relationship with another Facebook user and you are therefore engaged or married, then you can open the special page (go to the partner's profile, press the button with three applications and then see friendship details) to see all the photos and news about the couple. The page is the same as that of the normal profile, with the list of news about the couple, photos, mutual friends, and events.

Embed posts on another website

If you have a blog or website or if you participate in a forum, you can share anyone's status by embedding it as if it were a YouTube video.

This Facebook feature is only available for public posts. The option is visible in the menu that appears by pressing the down arrow to the right of a post. Facebook provides HTML code for you to copy and paste into the webpage to embed the post.

Check all the photos in which we are tagged so as not to make them appear on our profile timeline

In the settings, it is always important to activate the Facebook tag check to hide any photos that we are not interested in showing from the timeline. The option to change is to "check posts where friends tag you before they appear in your timeline".

Communicate through video chat

Not everyone knows that Facebook can make free video calls from your PC.

Schedule a meeting or special event

Facebook works really well both for inviting friends and for organizing private parties or meetings, for birthdays or invitations of various kinds. Since on Facebook there are all or almost all friends, it has really become the best tool on the internet to make private invitations to people and communicate to them the day, date, and place of a party or even a meeting.

CHAPTER 6

12 WAYS TO USE THE ALGORITHM TO YOUR BENEFIT

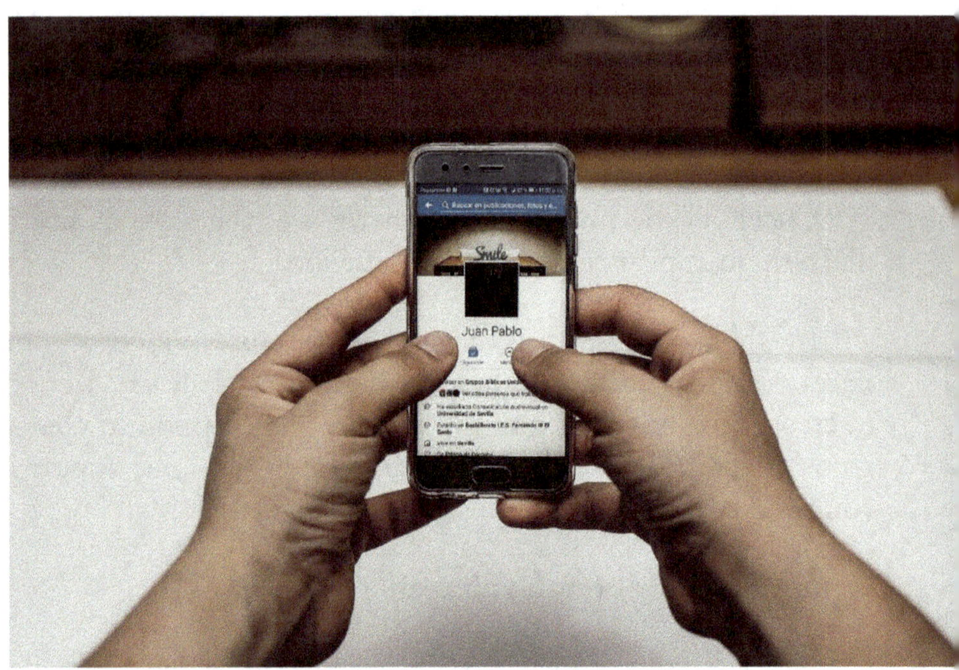

If you're wondering why your Facebook reach and interaction have decreased, you're not alone. The average reach of Facebook postings has decreased considerably since 2019.

For brands, this means that only 5.5 percent of their followers see organic posts. Even the most popular businesses with the most followers had lower averages. Why?

The explanation can be found in the way Facebook's algorithm operates. While Facebook's algorithm isn't the sole element influencing reach, it is unquestionably one of the most powerful. If you don't keep up with Facebook's algorithm updates, you'll have a more difficult time getting your posts seen by the individuals who are most important to your business.

In 2019, Facebook made a significant adjustment to its algorithm by providing users greater choice over what they see in their feed, as well as the option to see why a specific post is showing up in their feed.

Fortunately, even without the assistance of paid advertising, businesses can go a long way toward ensuring that their postings are seen by users.

This chapter will give you a fast introduction to how Facebook's algorithm works and how you may optimize it for your business.

How the Facebook Algorithm Works

Facebook's algorithm, like search engine algorithms, ranks all posts that have a chance to be shown on a user's news feed, based on the likelihood that they will have a positive reaction to the content.

Facebook prioritizes posts from friends over brands, emphasizing meaningful interactions.

The Facebook algorithm works in four steps to create the news feed:

It creates a list of all posts available for viewing.

Through specific signals, it understands what each post is about.

It makes predictions about how the user will react to each post on the list.

It creates a final score that will determine the order of posts on the feed.

Facebook's ranking factors are based on user behavior data and also take into account how everyone uses the platform. There are three main categories that Facebook looks at:

who users typically interact with;

the type of content: videos, images, links, and so on;

the popularity of the post.

Beginning in May 2019, Facebook began polling users directly to better understand the content they want to see. Facebook asked users for things like:

Who are your closest friends?

Which posts do you find most interesting?

Is this Facebook group important to you?

How interested are you in seeing the content of this page you follow?

Based on those responses, Facebook has updated its algorithm so that news will be better for users. This included showing users more content from groups and pages they had been following for the longest time or with more interest.

How to Use the Facebook Algorithm Effectively

It might appear that the changes to how Facebook's algorithms work were designed to make it harder for your brand posts to be seen without creating ads, and this may also be true. Facebook makes money from ads, after all, so it makes sense that they want to push brands in that direction.

But the people behind Facebook also know that showing users the content they don't really want to see is a surefire way to get them to leave the platform. This means businesses will be less likely to pay for ads as Facebook's audience would be smaller. So, let's assume it's a combination of things: Facebook wants users to be happy with what they see in their news feed while pushing corporate Facebook pages to create better and more relevant content if they want to reach users without making every post a paid ad.

Since Facebook's algorithm focuses on creating more authentic or meaningful interactions, your brand will need to create better content with the intention of fostering real interactions. But how?

Here are 13 ways you can make Facebook's algorithm work for your business.

Post content at the right time

Facebook's algorithm prioritizes the most engaging posts, so it's important to understand when your audience is online and most active, so you can post during those peak hours.

Use your Facebook page analytics tool to understand what time your followers are most active.

Post often and regularly

Companies that post consistently are more likely to get better engagement. Facebook's algorithm rewards frequency and well-done posts, so try to post high-quality content frequently. We highly recommend that you create a content calendar for Facebook so that you have your posts ready to use.

Focus on video content

In recent years, video content has become more and more popular. If you haven't started using video marketing yet, you should start right away. According to a study conducted by Wyzowl in 2020, 96% of people watched an explanatory video to learn more about a product or service, 84% of people say they were convinced to buy a product or service by watching a video of a brand, and 74% of people say they have been convinced to buy or download software or application by watching a video.

Facebook tweaked its algorithm to show more original, high-quality videos in users' news feeds. There are three ranking factors to consider when creating video content for Facebook:

Intention and loyalty: create videos that attract users over and over again.

Create interest: the video should be attractive enough to be watched by viewers for at least 12/15 seconds. Creating longer videos might bore your audience and your content wouldn't be watched in full.

Originality: like all social media platforms, Facebook prefers original content that isn't repurposed by other platforms.

Also, don't forget about the great Facebook Live. When you go live, your followers will be notified, which will definitely increase engagement.

Promote discussion instead of seeking compromise

You know those posts that your relatives always shared: "like it if you remember" or "comment on a number and I'll do it". Well, Facebook now penalizes companies that use the same tactics to get comments, tags, and likes.

This doesn't mean you should never do such posts (they can be an engaging way to poll your followers), however, Facebook wants to encourage creators to create discussions, rather than just asking followers to "like" something.

To guide the conversation, use questions and encourage discussion. Even if you don't want to post overly controversial content, there are ways to encourage debate on topics related to your business.

For example, an email marketing service provider may ask their followers for feedback on cold emails and hot emails.

Say "No" to clickbait and low-quality content

In addition to the engagement posts just mentioned, Facebook actively discourages clickbait as well. Clickbait uses uniquely designed links and thumbnails to grab attention and get clicks. Most of the time, clickbait is misleading or deceptive.

In addition to clickbait, there are other types of content that

Facebook disapproves of: misinformation and fake news;

content that is offensive but does not meet the banned content threshold;

links to sites that do not add value or contain stolen content;

misleading health information;

fake videos that have been reported by third-party fact-checkers.

Encourage employees and partners to share and engage

If you have employees or work with influencers on Facebook, you can clearly see how Facebook's algorithm works to use it to your advantage. Ask your employees and partners to share and interact with your content to help you stand out from other users' news.

Why does it work? Facebook prioritizes content from people you know personally, so you're more likely to see content from friends and family than posts from businesses you follow on the platform.

By asking your employees and partners to share your posts with their networks, your content will have greater reach. Plus, people are much more likely to read content from friends and family than your brand.

Focus on images and posts instead of links to external sites

It is no secret that Facebook wants to keep users on its platform instead of sending them to external sites. To this end,

Facebook minimizes posts with external links.

This doesn't mean that your posts with links pointing to your business site will never appear, but it does mean that you should have a mix of content, with an emphasis on native Facebook content and keeping users on the platform.

In addition to using native content, Facebook loves visual content. In fact, Facebook posts with images get significantly higher engagement than posts without images. Make sure you include a visual element (GIF, image, video, infographic, etc.) within each post so that you can use the Facebook algorithm to your advantage.

Create Facebook specific content

I told you about it briefly in the tip above, but we'll go into a little more detail here, as specific content created specifically for the platform is so important that it makes Facebook's algorithm happy.

Start by writing unique and engaging descriptions for your posts, even if you reuse content you've shared on Facebook previously. Don't share exactly the same. Change the content a bit to avoid being repetitive.

This doesn't just apply to post titles. You can use an image editing tool to turn posts into eye-catching images or turn posts into video content using a video editing tool.

Take advantage of Facebook groups

Facebook groups are one of the best ways to ensure that your followers see the content at the top of their news feed more often.

You can harness the power of Facebook groups by creating a new group for your brand. This group is a place to encourage discussion and provide product training, entertainment, user problem solutions, and other content that adds value to your followers.

Focus on the right (small) audience

Facebook offers great audience targeting tools that you can use to fine-tune who views your content. While it may seem counterintuitive to narrow your audience, you will see that engagement increases accordingly.

Greater engagement, in turn, means your content will be rewarded for the way Facebook's algorithm works and rank higher in users' news feeds.

Use Facebook Ads

Your organic (non-paid) content will go a long way in building and nurturing relationships with your audience, but we'd be remiss if we didn't include Facebook advertising as the best and fastest way to increase brand awareness on the platform.

By targeting and using the Facebook Pixel, you can reach exactly who you need to grow your audience. From there, you can better understand the type of content that works for the type of people you want to reach.

Facebook Ads has a great return on investment, which is why 93% of online marketers already use Facebook advertising.

When you combine Facebook advertising with the 10 tips we've already covered, you'll get even more out of your advertising efforts.

Using organic and paid efforts together is the best way to get your content in front of as many target audiences as possible, while still pushing your organic content to nurture the relationships you're starting.

Don't forget about Instagram

Facebook greatly values brands that also have a corporate Instagram account. In fact, the platform offers the possibility of connecting the two profiles to each other so as to be able to significantly expand their target audience.

If you haven't done so yet, then hurry up to create your page and find out how to increase your followers on Instagram right away.

Make Facebook's algorithm work for your brand

Facebook's algorithm is getting better and better at showing Facebook users only what they want to see. This is why it's so important to create high-quality Facebook content that will delight and engage your target audience.

Using the tips above, you will be able to know how Facebook's algorithm works and use it to your advantage, gaining new followers, improving visibility, and boosting your brand on the platform.

CHAPTER 7

HOW TO CREATE A COMPANY PAGE

Creating a business Facebook page is an important step that can open up great growth opportunities for anyone with a business to promote.

A company Facebook page, in fact, is a great way to communicate the value of a professional activity online, regardless of size.

It doesn't matter whether you have a company already started or you are a freelancer: having a well-structured and curated presence on Facebook is now essential. And maybe you already know.

Before getting to the heart of creating a company's Facebook page, let's make a very important premise.

Do not underestimate this question, because planning a strategy to follow right from the start will not only simplify your everyday life but will make you reach those goals for which it is actually worth being on Facebook.

For example, you could open your business Facebook page too:

• increase brand awareness, that is to be more visible and make yourself known;

• acquire new contacts and new customers;

• get to know your target audience better;

• sell your products;

• increase traffic to your site or blog.

There may be other goals that push you to create your page, the important thing is to have them clear right away and build your presence based on these goals.

Create Your Facebook Page

You can easily create your business Facebook page from your personal profile.

At the top of the blue bar on the right, next to your name,

click "Create": a window will open with various options. Immediately select "Page", and here you will find the first choice:

- How to create a business Facebook page: choose the type of page you want to create.

- After selecting "Get started", you will be asked for the name your page will have and the category of your company.

- When deciding on the name, I recommend that you actually choose the one that relates to your business or is easily recognizable by people.

- So, avoid confusing your audience by complicating the name by adding other terms and words.

- Now let's move on to the category - start typing your industry right away. Facebook will suggest a series of pre-set categories to choose from. Once you have selected your category, click on "Continue".

- Now your business Facebook page needs visual content to come to life. If you don't have your profile picture ready yet, skip this step, you can upload it later.

- Create a business Facebook page: choose your visual content carefully.

In general, you may want to upload your logo as a profile picture, or if you are a freelancer, a good idea is to choose a professional photo of yourself. Now Facebook asks you for the cover image. Again, you can possibly skip this step and come back to it later.

For the cover image Facebook offers you several interesting and creative options:

• a simple image that you can choose from your photos or upload a new one specially created;

• a video, which must be between 20 and 90 seconds and the recommended size of 820 x 462 pixels;

• a slideshow of images, that is a sort of browsable album.

Of course, once you've uploaded a cover image, you can change it at any time and even switch to a video or slideshow.

If the image you have chosen is not the optimal size, you can decide to keep it anyway and before saving it you can drag it to position it more correctly. Now your page is ready… or almost!

Add Important Information to Your Business Facebook Page

If you have followed the steps so far, you will now have your company's Facebook page in front of you. It's a bit empty at the moment, don't you think?

Click immediately on "Information" on the left side of the page, under your profile picture. The section dedicated to the information you are going to enter and that will be very important for your future followers will open.

Do not neglect this section: the more accurate you are, the easier it will become to be found even by those who do not yet know you.

Identify the keywords that best define your business and include them in the description.

Don't forget the section dedicated to your story, which you can find on the right in the information section.

It is a very interesting space that allows you to tell your audience, easily edit the text and insert photos and videos, as well as any other links. When you have finished, click on "Post" to make it immediately visible on the page.

Further down, under the story, you will also find the possibility of inserting the members of the team, that is, who will really take care of the page and who will be visible with their personal accounts.

Add a button

Adding the button is also a fundamental part because it is the first precise indication you will give to your audience, the first call to action. It will also be one of the main channels of direct communication with your audience.

You have a wide choice available:

• Bookings: you can choose to make appointments directly on Facebook or direct people to your website.

• Contact: select the type of contact you prefer. You can choose to be contacted directly on Facebook Messenger or to be reached by email or you can also ask people to join your mailing list.

• More information: it allows you to show a video both

internal and external to Facebook, or to direct people to your web page.

• Shop With You: if you want to sell online, this is the best option. You can also choose to direct people to your Facebook showcase.

• Download your app: people can download your app from your site or play it online.

When it comes to directing people to your website to have them take a specific action, like subscribing to your newsletter, don't link to your homepage. Avoid having your users take several steps because they probably won't do them eventually, or they'll leave the session.

Instead, insert a direct link to your landing page where you collect emails or sell your product.

Now that your business page is taking shape, let's take a look at other features that will be useful to you as well.

Settings

Check the "Settings" you find at the top right of your newborn page.

There are several sections that you might be interested in. Here I will tell you about the most useful ones, but I recommend that you take a look at all the features of the settings.

When you create your business Facebook page, settings are also very important: they allow you to keep your page under the control

From the "Settings" of your company's Facebook page, you can activate various useful features and also change the page template.

In the general settings, you will see the visibility of the page. In fact, you can decide that your page remains on standby for a while, perhaps to better refine the details and images. Just click on "Edit" and choose not to publish it or vice versa, when it is complete.

Check that all parts of the general settings satisfy you and go to "Messages".

In messages, you can easily change the way people contact you and you can also decide to send automatic messages to whoever writes to you.

Once in the section reserved for messages, take a look at the "Assistance with replies" part: here you can choose which automatic reply to send to the people who contact you on Messenger.

It is a practical solution especially if you already know that you will not be able to immediately reply to your future messages while you are busy. Facebook will do it for you and send the text you set by clicking on "Edit".

You may want to send a greeting, for example, along with your contact details and website, your opening hours, or other personalized messages that might be of interest to people.

You can also integrate Messenger directly on your website!

So, when your follower visits your site, they can chat with your Facebook page directly from there. In fact, the Messenger icon will be visible on your site.

To activate the feature, go to "Messenger Platform". Scroll to "Customer Chat Plug-in" and click "Configure".

Here you can customize the initial texts but also the colors so that they reflect your brand.

Remember that to integrate the chat on your site you should have a minimum of web development skills.

Once the configuration is complete, Facebook will provide you with the code to insert on your site.

You also have the option to send recurring messages to your users, i.e., "Subscription Messages". Check out Facebook's guidelines first.

Now let's move on to the "Templates" and "Tabs". Here it's easy to change the default page templates and linked structures.

Try changing the template and see which type of structure suits you best.

Usually, each model differs for the tabs, that is, for the most relevant areas that will be immediately visible to those who visit the page.

The tabs contain the most important sections, including posts, photos, videos, reviews, events, offers, and so on. Some tabs can be removed, such as reviews and events. You could actually opt for the latter choice but keep in mind that one day you can easily go back.

You can also add other tabs that you don't see present: just select "Use default tabs"> "No" and then choose "Add a Tab".

The Roles of the Page

By default, the creator of the page automatically becomes the administrator, i.e., you have full control of the page. However, you may want to assign different roles to other people who will help you with management. The roles you have available, in addition to the administrator, are:

- editor

- moderator

- advertiser

- analyst

Assigning the administrator role to someone else is never a good idea, especially from a security point of view.

If you want to get help in managing your page, assign the role of editor to that person by typing their account in the space provided.

If, on the one hand, you want to allow a collaborator to create paid ads and campaigns on Facebook and Instagram, you will assign him the role of the advertiser.

If, on the other hand, you just need to share the analytics related to the page, you will give that person the role of an analyst.

But how do you remove unwanted people from your business Facebook page? Until recently it was perhaps more intuitive to have an overview of the people who had liked your page.

Now you have a whole special section that you always find in "Settings"> "People" and other pages. From here you can eventually remove or block some haters, or simply those who are not on target with your business. Click on the wheel next to the name you are interested in.

A little further down you will find the part relating to Instagram, from which you can connect your existing account and create paid advertisements on both social platforms.

The Insights of Your New Business Facebook Page

At the moment this very important section will be empty because you have just created your page and consequently there is still no analytical data to show you.

Going forward, when you start publishing your posts or creating ads, insights will be the key free tool that Facebook makes available to you.

Thanks to the insights you will be able to understand which types of posts receive the most engagement and at what times your audience is more easily reachable.

You will also be able to check the actual reach of your posts, and compare organic and paid reach.

To build a strategy that will be useful to you over time, download the analytical data to study it in depth. Facebook allows you to download them to an Excel sheet by selecting the date range you are interested in.

When you manage your company's Facebook page you must always monitor the insights and the analytical data that Facebook makes available to you for free.

For now, let's see a general overview of your business Facebook page data.

The Insights Overview

Here you have an overall view of the progress of your page.

Actions performed by users deserve some attention. They include any clicks on the link you entered, your information, or the main call to action button.

Staying in this section, you can also decide to monitor and compare other Facebook pages of your competitors or similar to yours.

Select "Add Pages" to manually choose comparison pages.

See When Your Followers Are Online

To understand when it is best to publish a post, at what times, and on what days, go to "Post".

The graph that opens clearly shows you the general reach peaks depending on the hours, but also on the days of the week.

From here you can also choose the "Post Types" tab which

will show you which post types (images, videos, or others) get the most reach, the most clicks, and the most reactions.

Of course, until you publish consecutively over a certain period of time, all of this data will be scarce or even empty. To get a demographic profile of your fans instead, go to "People". You will then see the percentage of women and men who follow your page and in which geographical area they reside.

Who views your page?

Another statistic I recommend that you monitor is the one related to "Page Views".

The data refer to both users logged in to Facebook and to an external users, i.e., people who view the page without having logged in, perhaps because they arrived at your page through other channels.

With the views you can also understand which section is visited the most and also from which device.

There are other data that you can discover in the views but unfortunately, you must first acquire a certain number of followers to be collected.

The organic reach of your page

Organic reach should be the heart of your page somewhat.

At present, it is more of a chimera, and you should definitely not rely on it alone to decree whether or not your goals have been achieved.

If once, until a few years ago, it could perhaps have been based on organic reach, now Facebook for companies is very much based on paid ads.

On the other hand, the amount of content that is placed on the global platform every day makes it increasingly difficult for you to bring out the posts of your page in the newsfeed of your fans.

So, how to behave? Surely a series of beautiful images and videos, even and especially the live ones, continue to have good reach, especially if you analyze the insights related to the posts.

That said, it would be a good idea to start creating a monthly advertising program based on the goals you want to achieve.

To grow your page, I want to give you 3 tips:

Avoid the exchange of likes like the plague! There are many Facebook groups dedicated to like exchanges, advertising exchanges, and so on. At first, they may seem like a nice gimmick, but after a while, you will realize that you are wasting your energy for nothing. And your reach will plummet...

Avoid inviting all your friends to like your page without criteria! Only invite people you know are targeting your business and page.

Don't fall into the vanity metrics trap! The vanity metrics can give you a smile today but hardly the salary at the end of the month... so, based only on concrete results and not on the likes that your post receives.

CHAPTER 8

HOW TO MANAGE A COMPANY PAGE

In this chapter, I'll describe what managing a Facebook page for a company comprises, how it works, and what it's for in the simplest terms possible.

I won't get into why Facebook is so popular or how to create a profile; everyone understands this by now. I'd like to show you how you, too, can use this channel to market your business; you'll learn what it takes to bring it online, as well as the expenses and timelines involved. Above all, we'll look at the measures to take before creating a company Facebook page.

Finally, you will learn whether Facebook is beneficial to your business and what objectives you can attain.

Every day, I chat with entrepreneurs about social strategy; when it comes to social media, the mind automatically visualizes Facebook, because it was the first and is still the most popular today.

Knowing Facebook is taken for granted, but not everyone realizes the subtle distinction between using it for leisure and for work.

When I presented an introduction course for the autonomous administration of social platforms, they virtually laughed in my face, saying, "but I know how to use Facebook."

Okay, we all know how to use it, but... what does Facebook mean for your business? What are your objectives? Are you reaching out to them?

Only then did the entrepreneur learn that simply existing on social media is insufficient for effective communication.

Today, Facebook is the best communication platform for many activities (Note: I said many, not all.) We will see later for those who are not suitable for Facebook) for the following reasons:

It's easy to use

There are many people (even your customers)

You can target audiences and spend in relation to the needs of your business

What Is Facebook for Your Business?

Depending on the activity, you can set different goals, here are the most common:

Communicate with your customers or prospects

Promote your products or services

Retain your customers and make you remember

Increase the reputation and awareness of your company

Do after-sales assistance

Collect reviews or comments on your products and services

Stimulate word of mouth

Does It Make Sense for Your Business to Be on Facebook?

If you want to achieve one of the goals written above, Facebook could be for you. But there are still a few things to ask:

Is your target on Facebook?

Do you have something to say to your target that can be used on Facebook?

Do you have time and/or financial resources to dedicate?

If you answered yes to all 3 questions, then you are ready to launch on social media! Not sure about the answers you gave? I'll give you some examples:

Example 1: I am an ice cream maker from a big city.

- Is your target on Facebook? My ideal clients are men and women aged 13 to 60 who live in my neighborhood and love sweets. Yes, they are definitely on Facebook.

- Do you have something to say to your target that can be used on Facebook? Ice cream and food, in general, are very popular online, I could talk about the ingredients, and show pictures of the ice cream sundaes, my satisfied customers, and the staff at work. Yes, I have content.

- Do you have time and/or financial resources to dedicate? I can devote 1 hour a day to creating and sharing content, plus I'll take a course to improve the strategy and dedicate some sponsorship budget. I will devote time and money.

Activating an online business for your business will most likely be the right choice and you will have many positive results.

Example 2: I am the owner of a company that produces presses in a small town.

• Is your target on Facebook? My clients are entrepreneurs or department heads from my country and from abroad, mostly men from 35 to 70 years old. Probably some of them, especially the younger ones, have a Facebook profile. Some of my clients or potential clients are on Facebook.

• Do you have something to say to your target that can be used on Facebook? There are many topics to be covered. The pressing topic, however, is not one of the most discussed on social media. I probably wouldn't have a very large audience to speak to. The topic does not lend itself to social media.

• Do you have time and/or financial resources to dedicate? I don't have time to dedicate to following the channel and creating the content, I could entrust this task to the girl from the administration. If it goes well, we will try to do paid advertising. I will not spend time and money.

With these premises, the chances of success are minimal. The sector does not have much appeal on social media, moreover, if the task is entrusted to someone who is not qualified and without an adequate budget, the experiment will have little chance of success.

Returning to us, if you have decided to land on Facebook with your company you must know that upon registration you will not have to create a profile, but a page.

You have to be very careful because only with a fan page you can register as a company, you will also have the possibility to create paid advertisements, which is impossible for personal profiles.

How to Open a Facebook Page

Opening a Facebook page is easy thanks to a step-by-step guided procedure. Once logged in with your profile, connect to this link: https://www.facebook.com/pages/creation/,

choose the category that best suits your band, enter the name and address (if you have a physical location), and a brief description of the activity.

Remember that the username of the page is the one preceded by the sign. Example: @juliagasp, it cannot be changed until it reaches 200 likes.

71

In the following steps, you will have to insert the profile photo, for example, the logo, the cover photo, the photo of the company, or of one of your advertising campaigns.

At this point, the page will be created, go to the settings to complete all the details: hours, telephone number, long description, and so on.

Structure of a Facebook Page

The Facebook page has a variable structure, the social network is in fact constantly updated to ensure that the user gets bored as little as possible.

The basic elements of a page are:

Cover: this can be a photo, video, or slideshow. It's important because it's the first thing a new user sees about your company. As you know, the first impression is very important. Insert quality images that make it clear what you do and what your strong point is.

Profile image: if you manage a company page, here you will need to insert the logo photo, if you manage the page of a public figure, you can insert a portrait. This image must be square and with a high level of visibility, because it is also displayed very small.

Timeline: the central part is occupied by the posts of the page, that is, all the content you have published over time. Remember that the posts are displayed in chronological order, but you have the option to pin a featured post, so as to give relevance to some strategic content.

Page numbers: the page numbers are listed in the right section, i.e., the "likes", the people who follow you, the people who have been physically in your company, and the pages you like.

Call To Action button: under the cover image it is possible to activate a button to indicate the action to be performed by the user. Here it is necessary to insert a link, for example to the home page of the site, to the sales page, to the e-commerce section, and so on. It all depends on the strategy you want to adopt.

Information section: this is to be seen as a "Contacts" page, there are addresses, timetables, maps, information on services, costs, menus, and so on.

Photos and videos: all the photos and videos published on the page are presented. They are divided into photos or videos from the timeline, photos published by applications (e.g., shared by Instagram), and thematic albums (e.g., team photos, photos of an event, etc.).

Events: each page has the possibility to create events. They are small pages with all the information relating to an event. They must have a start and end date and interested people can decide whether to participate. This page lists all the events held by the company, past, and future.

Community: each user has the possibility to publish content on your page. This content will have very low visibility, but it will all be gathered on this page. It's useful for understanding what your audience thinks and getting ideas for improvements or new services.

Information and Ads: in this section Facebook shows the active advertisements for the page. This is a feature released in June 2018 to improve transparency on the platform.

Reviews: This is one of the most important sections on the business side, your current customers can express their opinion through the evaluation in stars and by writing a comment. Having positive reviews is important for improving page visibility and increasing trust in potential customers.

How to Create a Facebook Post

The types of posts that can be created are really many. We can publish videos, photos, and slideshows, tell how we feel, register in a place, support a non-profit cause, communicate the achievement of a goal, promote a product, create an event, and so on.

The 3 pieces of content that work best are:

1. Photo or multi-photo post with the related caption

2. Post with video or photo slideshow with caption

3. Link to the website with inherent image and caption reasons to visit the link

Once the post has been created, you can save it as a draft, schedule it in the future or in the past (by choosing the date and time) or publish it immediately.

The Roles of the Facebook Page

When you create a Facebook page the only one who can publish is you, that is the profile with which you created the page.

Very often the page has to be managed by several people, for example, your collaborators.

For this, you can go to the "Settings panel" -> "Page Roles" and add the new person by entering the name and surname with which she is registered on Facebook or by email address.

You can assign each user different roles, depending on which they will have more or less freedom of action within the page.

The most privileged role is the administrator, then there is the editor, the moderator, the advertiser, and the analyst.

Remember that the administrator can manage the roles of the page and thus remove you from management.

Congratulations, you have created your page! And now? Now you need to build a strategy based on the content and goals you want to achieve.

The Editorial Calendar

Get a weekly calendar. Choose how many posts you want to do per week. Choose what kind of post you want to make on that particular day and what goal you want to achieve. Decide if and how much you want to invest in advertising.

Editorial calendar example: I am a dog food manufacturer.

I want to create 3 posts per week (Tuesday, Thursday, and Saturday). The contents of the posts are:

healthy nutrition recipe

photo of a dog sent by customers

promotion of a product.

The goals are:

increase the visibility of the brand;

stimulate word of mouth;

build customer loyalty.

For the first month, I will allocate 100 dollars for advertising.

What to Post on the Facebook Page?

Are you in a content crisis? Here's what you need to do to not go into abstinence:

• Follow your competitors, what do they do? What are they talking about?

• What problems do your customers have? Try to solve them using social media.

• Stimulate interaction by talking to them, they will give you interesting ideas.

• Keep always up to date. You are the reference point for your sector, you need to know everything and disclose it to position yourself as an expert.

Attention: Watch out for Personal Branding! Many entrepreneurs understand the potential of social media but do not have time to follow them, so they entrust the management of the pages to others. At the same time, they use their social profiles recklessly, not thinking that for the end customer, the entrepreneur profile and the company page are on the same level.

Managing your image through a strategy is called personal branding. If you have a company or a shop, you are known by everyone for being the owner. Your image, especially online, must be taken care of in such a way that it does not harm your company.

Always pay attention to what you post or share, all your customers will associate it with your company.

Who Sees Your Facebook Page Posts?

If you have a Facebook page already active you will have noticed that the posts you publish are not seen by all users on Facebook, not only that, not even by all the people who have liked your page.

You need to know that the biggest revenue on Facebook is given by paid sponsorships, which is why it limits the visibility of your posts so that you are forced to invest some budget to reach your target. On average a post is seen by 6% of the subscribers of the page, a percentage destined to decrease.

Furthermore, the heart of Facebook is composed of its algorithm, which is an automatic process that reacts differently depending on the content you post.

Trivializing a lot: the more your audience likes a piece of content, the more views it can have.

The approval rate is established by the algorithm that analyzes thousands of factors. For this reason, if you want to use Facebook for your company you have to respect 2 rules:

create quality content that your audience likes;

invest in sponsorships.

These are the rules of the game.

What Time to Post on Facebook

One of the factors that Facebook analyzes to decide whether to reward the visibility of your post is the percentage of people interacting within seconds of publication.

When you post content, Facebook shows it to some people, depending on their reactions it will decide whether to show it to others or not.

That's why it's important to post when you have the best chance of your audience being online.

There are times of day when the public is most active, for example in the morning before starting work, at lunchtime, and in the evening.

The best thing, however, is to understand when your

audience is online. Thanks to the analysis tools you can do it.

Go to the "Insight" -> "Posts" section, here you can see day by day when people interacted with your posts and peak times. Try posting the half-hour before the peak of users.

Increase the Number of Followers on Your Facebook Page

There are several ways to increase the likes of your page. In order to get good results, it is best to test them and check which ones work best for you.

Here are some strategies:

• **Sponsor**: Facebook offers the possibility to promote your page for a fee, showing it to a potentially interesting target.

• **Social icons**: insert the social icons and the suggestion to like all your communication material (website, business card, point of sale, other social networks, and so on).

• **Use your profile**: you have the option to invite all your friends to like the page you manage. Try not to add everyone indiscriminately but only those who may be genuinely interested.

• **Community**: take advantage of the network to make yourself known, intervene in a coherent and polite manner in Facebook groups, comment on blogs, become active on other social networks, and write to pages similar to you. Attention, you must not spam but create relationships.

• **Go viral:** one of the most effective strategies, but also the most difficult one is being able to make content go viral.

This means that a lot of people see your post and are forced to share it on their profiles. For this to happen the content must be special. E.g., funny videos, contests, real-time marketing, fake news, and so on.

Facebook User Data

Facebook is currently the most used social network in the world, here are the numbers in January 2018:

number of active users per month: 2,200,000,000;

number of active users per day: 1,450,000,000;

the social network most used in North and South America, Europe, Africa, India, Oceania, and Southeast Asia.

Facebook Costs for Companies

As we have seen so far, Facebook provides the creation of profiles and pages for free. To date, you can create all kinds of content you want in an unlimited number.

Facebook thrives on user content so it will never limit them.

Facebook is free, but its management is not.

Here are some of the costs you face if you want to make the most of Facebook for your business:

your time;

web marketing consultant or ads expert for strategy and sponsorship;

budget for post sponsorship;

photographer or videomaker for the creation of quality content;

social media manager or copywriter for post creation and publication;

training courses, books;

management or analysis software.

Remember that all of these costs are monthly and ongoing. Depending on your skills you can have more or less professional involvement in the management of the page.

On average, a Facebook page for a small professionally managed business has a minimum cost of 500 dollars per month.

How to Promote a Company on FB

Knowing how to promote a Facebook page is essential for a return on business.

First off, you need to know that each post you publish can be sponsored, i.e., shown as an advertisement to a certain number of users.

When promoting a post, you can choose the most suitable audience (age, place, gender, interests, ethnicity) and set a budget.

The more you invest, the more people will see the post. But it's not that simple.

Depending on the quality of the post, Facebook will reward or penalize it in terms of visibility. E.g., if your audience likes a post, you could spend 0.02 dollars per view, if you don't like it, the cost could go up to 0.20 dollars. With the same total budget, e.g., 10 dollars the post you don't like will be shown to fewer people. 500 people for the good post, 50 people for the bad post.

Anyone can easily sponsor on Facebook, but my advice is to be very careful.

If you are clear about your goals and don't know how to measure the results, you could be spending money unnecessarily.

CHAPTER 9

ADVERTISEMENT ON FACEBOOK ADS

Facebook is currently the social network with the most active users on the planet. That is why we cannot afford to pass up the opportunity to promote on Facebook.

Talking about this social media's stats is talking about its triumphs. There will be 2701 million active users in October 2020, which is a huge number.

Facebook Ads are a popular kind of online marketing. The

fact that most businesses bet on Facebook Ads is neither a trend nor a coincidence. Many people utilize Facebook Ads to grow their Instagram following.

Ads may be fully tailored, and thanks to the information that social media platforms have on their users, campaigns directed at specific audiences can be created. As a result, betting on this type of campaign can lead to success.

What exactly is advertising on Facebook Ads?

Launching a Facebook advertising campaign entails publicizing your organization, service, or product on social media. You may easily build an appealing Facebook ad using the publishing tools.

A message that contains an eye-catching photograph or video will be enough to pique your audience's curiosity. If you've used other online advertising methods, such as Google AdWords, you'll see that the format is nearly identical.

Advertising on Facebook necessitates a financial investment as well as a message to convey to your target demographic. At the same time, while it is possible to produce sponsored posts that are targeted to all social media users, it is preferable to have a well-defined audience in order to segment the campaign and achieve the greatest results.

Why Should Your Business Advertise on Facebook?

There are many reasons that could make you consider a Facebook advertising strategy. Actually, advertisements created through Facebook Ads have a lot of benefits you should know:

<u>**Audience segmentation**</u>. Thanks to all the data Facebook has about users it's very easy to segment the ad you want to create.

<u>**Making a post go viral**</u>. Even if you pay to advertise on Facebook, users can share your post among their contacts. This allows you to have a greater impact depending on the behavior of your potential customers.

<u>**Interaction**</u>. In addition to promoting your products and services, you can also launch interactive publications that allow you to gather important data about your audience. For example, a giveaway for a subsequent lead generation campaign.

<u>**Price**</u>. Advertising on Facebook is cheap and I'm not talking about money... Facebook with its tools is able to make you achieve the best result at the lowest price.

<u>**Measurement**</u>. Almost everyone who spends money on advertising wants to understand how it is spent and measure its effectiveness. Advertising on Facebook will be really easy thanks to its integrated and completely free statistics panel.

What Types of Advertising Are There on Facebook?

Almost anything can be promoted on Facebook. From an external page to an app, event, or even a specific place. However, before launching an ad on Facebook it is important to define what the ultimate goal of the advertisement is. Only then can you correctly decide the payment formula and the type of campaign you need.

Depending on your goals, you should use one type of Facebook advertising or another. You also need to define whether to pay per click (PPC) or per impression (PPI).

PPC is ideal if you intend to generate traffic on Facebook or a third-party site to look for visits or conversions. PPI is more suitable if you want to improve the visibility of your brand in general. Before explaining how to advertise on Facebook effectively, there are four things that you need to make clear right away otherwise your campaigns will most likely not work:

The structure of the campaigns

What the customer wants

The stage of the sales funnel

The Facebook pixel

To get the most out of your campaigns, I also recommend that you learn more about how the Facebook algorithm works.

Structure of Facebook advertising campaigns

The first thing you need to understand is how Facebook advertising is structured.

When you create your first ad you will see that three layers are created:

Ad campaign

Ad group

Ad

At each level, you will have to define different elements.

Regarding the campaign, we will tell Facebook what is the goal we want to achieve.

Levels of customer awareness

Understanding a customer's different levels of awareness is essential when planning advertising campaigns. Why is it so important? Because depending on what stage you are in, you will have to create some ads or others.

A customer can be found in five stages:

- Unaware of the problem

- Aware

- Aware of the solution

- Aware of the product

- Very aware

This is directly related to the conversion funnel, which is the next point.

The stage of the sales funnel

As in the previous case, depending on what stage of the funnel a person is in, a series of advertisements or others must be shown. Do you think we can impact people who don't know us in the same way at all? No.

Depending on where you are, you will have to show one piece of content or another. Check out this example.

In the first step, you need to show the content to raise awareness of an issue. In the MOFU phase, the goal will be to convert potential customers into leads. While in the last phase we will have to transform them into buyers. The acronym "MOFU" stands for Middle of Funnel and is the stage through which users who had reacted to the shown ads are qualified.

The Facebook pixel

All the campaigns we carry out must be able to measure and track them. As they say, anything that is not measured cannot be improved upon.

Thanks to the Facebook Pixel we will be able to measure all the conversions that take place on our site. Not only that, but it will also allow us to create custom audiences.

Create an Advertising Campaign on Facebook

The first step before beginning any campaign is to develop your Facebook advertising strategy. There are no results until there is a strategy.

Before you begin building your first Facebook campaign, make certain that you have well comprehended all of the preceding elements.

The first step is to open the Ads Manager. If you have not yet created an ad, you will see "No campaign" and a "Create" button. You can either click there or travel to the left, where there is also a green button.

When you click the button, you will see the three levels of advertising on Facebook:

Ad campaigns

Ad group

Ads

Facebook campaign name: [Device] - [Product] - [Goal].

This is a point that is usually overlooked and the first name that comes to mind is given. Error!

When you create a large number of Facebook advertising campaigns, it will be more difficult to find and search for previously created campaigns.

That is why it is important to always follow the same type of nomenclature. A good way to name them is with the following structure:

Facebook campaign name: [Device] - [Product] - [Goal].

This way you can filter based on the products you are promoting or the chosen goal.

Which Facebook Ads goal to choose

Depending on our goal, Facebook will optimize our ads to show them to the people who are most likely to reach them.

For example, if I select the "Traffic" goal, Facebook will look for people who are most likely to click on the links. If I choose "Video views", the ads will be shown to the people most likely to watch the videos.

The objectives are divided into the three main stages of a

sales funnel:

Notoriety

Consideration

Conversion

We will see in detail what the Facebook Ads goals are.

• <u>**Brand awareness**</u>: the goal of brand awareness is to show your Facebook ads to those people who are most likely to remember them. One of the variables that are used to measure this factor is the time people spend looking at an ad.

• <u>**Reach**</u>: the reach goal shows your ad to as many people as possible from the audience you created. It's a good option for running retargeting campaigns on Facebook and trying to impact those undecided people as many times as possible.

• <u>**Traffic**</u>: are you planning on getting as many visits to your website as possible or increasing the number of people using your app? If your goal is to increase web traffic, this may be the best option.

• <u>**Interactions**</u>: the goal of the interaction is usually one of the most used and mainly serves to increase interactions with your content. Here you can choose between interaction with the publication, "like", comments, "share", page likes, responses to events, and so on.

• <u>**App installations**</u>: Facebook will search your target audience for people who are inclined to download your app.

- **<u>Video views</u>**: this is a recommended type of advertising for launching new products and/or services. It is also perfect for increasing brand recognition and conveying more closeness to your audience

- **<u>Lead generation</u>**: Facebook Lead Capture Ads are a great type of campaign to get potential customers at a low price. If you have a page that doesn't convert, this may be the best option.

- **<u>Messages</u>**: this is a good option to start conversations in Messenger with those people who are undecided about buying your product and/or service and who need answers to their latest questions.

- **<u>Conversions</u>**: Facebook will look for those people who are most likely to convert depending on your goal. If your goal is to sell on Facebook, this could be the ideal goal. It also works very well for generating leads.

- **<u>Selling catalog products</u>**: this option is ideal if you have an online store, as it allows you to upload your product catalog and advertise to those who visit it.

- **<u>Point of sale traffic</u>**: used to advertise to those close to your business to try and get them to your physical store.

Traffic goal or conversion goal?

Traffic campaigns are optimized to show your ads to people who are more likely to click on our ads.

In conversion campaigns, your campaigns will be shown to the people most likely to convert (purchase or lead).

Before choosing the goal, ask yourself what you want to get from your ad, and remember to study a proper marketing strategy before starting.

A/B Test: What is it and what is it for?

Through A/B testing we can test different versions of the ads and see what works best. One of the keys to effective Facebook advertising is to do several tests and optimize.

The five variables you can choose:

Audience

Optimization of the publication

Placements

Contents

Ad group

How to optimize your Facebook Ads campaign budget

The next step will be to define how to optimize the Facebook campaign budget. Now Facebook allows you to optimize it at the campaign level. What does it mean?

It is the social network itself that is responsible for distributing among the ad sets that perform best.

You can set up your budget in two ways: daily and total.

The last step will be choosing the bidding strategy for the campaign.

By default, the lowest cost offer will be flagged, which means FB will try to optimize your budget to automatically get the best possible results.

If this is your first time running a campaign or you are inexperienced, I recommend that you leave this option selected.

Ad Group

Once you have finished the initial phase of creating your first Facebook Ads campaign, you will move on to the second step: the ad group. Within this phase you can set a series of parameters, you can choose the audience, the placements, and much more.

At this point, the first thing to do is define the name of the Ad Group.

Remember this is where we will define who to show the ads to. What I recommend is to include the type of audience in the nomenclature. The structure I like to use is:

· [N°] - [Type of traffic] - [Segmentation].

For example: 1 - TF - Visitors page X [7 days]. This way, it will be easier to measure which type of audience works best for you.

Facebook ad optimization

By optimizing ad serving, we will tell FB what we want to achieve.

For example, if in the campaign objective we select the

objective "Traffic", we can choose between:

Click on the link

Landing page views

Single daily reach

Impression

If we select "Click on the link", Facebook will search for people who are most likely to click. By choosing "Landing Page Views", you will try to find the ones that are most likely to click and load your webpage.

Dynamic content

Just above, I told you that one of the keys to optimizing campaigns is to test different ad versions. Through the dynamic content, we will give FB different combinations of:

Images

Videos

Titles

Descriptions

Call to Action

This way, Facebook will automatically show the variations and ultimately allocate more budget to the winning option.

Budget and planning

In the calendar part, we can define a start date and an end date. But how do choose the best audience for Facebook advertising?

The first thing you need to know is that there are different types of audiences. Depending on what your goal is, you will need to choose a suitable and studied segmentation.

Ideally, create several ad groups with multiple audiences and then see which one works best. If you underestimate this part, your campaigns will be a complete failure.

The three types of audiences on Facebook are:

Saved

Custom

Similar

Saved Audience

The saved audience is a real manual segmentation of our audience. The parameters we can work with are our place, age, sex, language, interests, behaviors, and type of connection.

Custom Audience

Through custom audiences, we can show ads to people who already know us or have interacted with us.

Remember that to create certain audiences, you must have the Facebook Pixel installed and configured correctly.

Similar audience

Through a similar audience, Facebook will look for people who look like your custom audience. Can you imagine looking for people who look like your customers in minutes? You can do it.

Positioning

When deciding how much to invest in Facebook Ads, you need to take into account the positioning of your ads to optimize your budget. The placement of these will depend on the type of campaign you have previously selected.

Depending on your goal, you'll have a series of ticks enabled or not, so don't be alarmed if sometimes not all of them appear.

By default, they will all appear as marked, but if you have a low budget to invest, I recommend that you don't select all locations.

On devices, you can decide whether to advertise to all or filter by PC or mobile.

While in the locations you can choose between:

- Feed

- Stories

- In-stream

- Messages

- Articles

- Apps and websites

If you intend to use the videos, I recommend that you click on

«only with Wi-Fi connection». Many users don't play videos on mobile connections because they don't want to waste data so keep this in mind.

Create the Facebook Ads Advertisements

We come to the last point, now we need to create the actual ad.

When it comes to creating effective Facebook ads, the first thing you need to know is what the structure is like.

The elements that I consider most important are:

- Image or video

- Text in the image

- Ad text

- Title of the ad

- Description

- Call to Action

When it comes to writing Facebook ad copy, there are several elements that we need to give more importance to.

We need to show the right message to the right people, at the right time, and for that, we need to know how to communicate with our target audience.

Name of the ad

I've seen accounts that give all kinds of names to ads. Think that in each ad set you will have at least three creatives (depending on your budget you can have more or less). So, when it comes to knowing which ads work best, the nomenclature needs to be clear as well. Personally, I also like to number them.

Facebook Ads advertising formats

We can choose between five types of Facebook advertising formats:

Image: the most used format for advertising on Facebook.

Videos: they make your ads more engaging.

Carousel: perfect for showing up to 10 items in a single listing.

Interactive experience: it highlights your products or brand with a full-screen experience.

Collection: perfect for showing a range of products from a catalog within the same ad.

The creativity of the ad

Good creativity can account for 70-90% of the success or failure of a Facebook ad. Take the time to create truly effective images or videos.

Pay attention to the text you add to the creatives! Facebook doesn't like text in ads at all. It can even stop showing your ads if they contain too much text or at least charge you more to reach the same people. That is why it is essential to check the text.

Copy of the Facebook ad

Through the image, we must attract people's attention, but it will be with our words that we will guide our potential customers to take the action we want.

When writing ad copy, you need to consider things like:

- What is the goal we want to achieve?

- At what stage of the sales funnel the person is?

- What audience are you targeting?

Review and post

We have reached the last step. Check that the Facebook Pixel is marked (to be able to measure everything) and press "Post". Now it will be only Facebook to review our campaign and activate it.

The campaign will go into the "Analysis phase". Once approved, the campaign will begin to be shown to people and will be active, but the ad group will be in the "Learning phase". Once you have achieved the first results, Facebook will be able to optimize your ad.

Don't worry if the first results are too expensive. Wait some time and then consider the changes you need to make to improve performance.

How to Advertise on Facebook Ads to Get Leads

Now I'll show you how to run a Facebook ad campaign to get more leads. The steps you need to do are the same as we did before.

The first thing we need to do is select the campaign goal. In this case, since it is a campaign to get contacts, we can use the objectives:

- Traffic

- Contact generation

- Conversions

And now what we will need to do is name the campaign with the same format we have used so far.

Create ad group

It's time to create your ad group, so the first thing you need to be clear about is which audience is right for a lead capture campaign.

In my case, I choose to show my ads to people who don't know me yet.

For this, I will mainly use two types of audiences: similar audiences and interest-based or behavioral audiences.

Some types of similar audiences I could create could be similar to my subscribers, my clients, and visitors to my website.

I could also create custom audiences of those people who

have visited my site in the past 30, 60, or 90 days and exclude my current subscribers.

Create your contact ad

For the last step remember to use different images and text to perform the A/B test and, depending on the variation, give it a name or another. One of the keys to getting customers to subscribe to your blog or newsletter is to use good copy and offer something in return.

In order for people to sign up and leave their email, you then need to offer them an interesting value proposition.

They both start with an affirmative question in which if you are interested in that proposal, you will always answer yes. Both include the free word throughout the ad.

If you have a blog and want to get more subscribers, I would consider this type of structure.

How to create effective Facebook advertising

When we are browsing a social network and we see a sponsored one, what is the first thing that catches our attention? The ad image or video, right?

That's right, this is the first thing we look at, so the first thing we need to do is create an attractive image that draws attention to the naked eye. For this, it is recommended to use a different color than the Facebook wall because otherwise, your ad will go unnoticed.

In addition to the image, a copy is essential to convince your prospect that you have an interesting value proposition and that they will be able to solve their problems. This is why the first is essential to know the audience we are addressing. Highlight the benefits of your product or service.

Here I have summarized all the tips you can use to write effective copy:

- Start with affirmative questions

- Arouse curiosity and interest

- Highlight the benefits

- Use lists

- Always use a Call to Action

- Add words like "free"

- Make an interesting value proposition

Starting with a positive inquiry is a popular and effective tactic.

Include a Call to Action that emphasizes the overall message and pushes the reader to perform the desired action.

CTAs can take the following forms:

- Buy now

- Find out more

- Request now

- Subscribe

- Contact us

CHAPTER 10

HOW MUCH DO FACEBOOK ADS COST?

One of the most efficient marketing techniques is to use Facebook Ads to sponsor and promote your ecommerce.

The majority of entrepreneurs, large and small, use Facebook Ads to gain clients and scale their businesses. In reality, over 1.6 billion people worldwide are in contact with a small business via Facebook.

What did Will Facebook Ads cost in 2021?

Well, that's a difficult issue to answer because there are so many variables involved, and depending on your situation, Facebook Ads might cost many dollars per click or as little as a few bucks.

So, how do you figure out how much Facebook Ads will cost you before you get in, so you can start using this method to market your ecommerce?

In this chapter, we will look at some industry standards that have been updated for 2021, how Facebook Ads function and how to utilize Facebook Ads, what the main aspects that influence the cost are, and what the methods are to lower it.

According to existing research, the cost of a Facebook ad for most businesses ranges between 0.50 and 2.00 dollars per click.

Let's take a deeper look at two of the more extensive studies we found on WordStream and AdEspresso to get a better understanding of how much Facebook Ads cost.

According to AdEspresso, the average CPC for Facebook Ads in September 2020 was $0.39.

Wordstream is less positive and claims it is 1.72 dollars. However, this is the industry average, and not everyone has to pay that much to use Facebook Ads.

The finance and insurance industries, for example, have the highest average, at $3.77 per click.

Others, such as fashion (0.45 USD per click), travel and tourism (0.63 USD), and retail (0.70 USD), have substantially lower Facebook advertising expenditures.

CPC Wordstream on Facebook Ads

Now, why is it that the average cost per click in 2019 is so low, even less than 0.45 dollars, according to AdEspresso?

The Covid-19 outbreak most likely affected the price of 2020, causing concern among many entrepreneurs who had to lower their advertising spending for the year. As a result, ad costs were lowest from March 2020 to September 2020.

It is possible to anticipate a similar situation in 2022, with prices growing but remaining limited due to economic difficulties.

Keep in mind that these averages should not be taken at face value. However, now that we have some ballpark statistics, we can look more closely at how to calculate how much Facebook Ads cost.

Let's begin by figuring out how this online advertising system works.

What Is the Process of Using Facebook Ads?

Let's look at how Facebook Ads campaigns and ad management function.

First and foremost: What exactly are Facebook Ads? Facebook adverts are sponsored messages from businesses that allow them to reach the people who are most important to them (audience). Advertisers build campaigns with certain goals in mind and then create ads inside those campaigns to assist them in achieving those goals.

Ads can display in the "News Feed" on desktop or mobile, as well as in the right column of Facebook on desktop, and on Instagram as Instagram Ads in the feed and in Stories. Advertisers may set all campaign aspects, from public words to pictures, conduct A/B tests, and much more, all through the dedicated Facebook Business Suite portal (formerly Facebook Business Manager).

Real auctions determine whether or not an advertisement displays on Facebook at a certain time and in the feed of a given person.

If Facebook hounded users with adverts, it is very likely that they would abandon the network. As a result, Facebook addresses this issue by restricting the amount of advertising that each user sees.

In other words, the available inventory is limited, and there are many people who want to use it to expand their business.

That is why you cannot simply pay and create a Facebook Ads ad to ensure that users see it.

Advertisers must instead bid to get an ad space. Simply said, it is an auction in which the highest bidder wins the placement and can show their ad to their target audience.

When you utilize Facebook Ads for your ecommerce, you are not simply vying for advertising space with your competitors. You're also up against anyone else who wants to target a similar market niche to yours.

Assume you sell women's clothes to young millennials who are concerned about their health.

You will not be competing with only other apparel businesses in this circumstance.

You will also be competing with chemical-free make-up brands, vegan product brands, local gyms looking for new members, nutrition coaches advertising food plans, and any other businesses targeting the same customer demographic.

When you create ads on Facebook, you'll see that the size of your audience changes every time you add a new targeting parameter.

Facebook Ads News for 2022

The year 2021 was a hectic one for all digital firms, and Facebook/Instagram was no exception. We've noticed notable changes throughout the Zuckerberg ecosystem, notably in relation to ads and the platform backend for marketers. Here are some of the most significant changes in 2021 that will have an impact on Facebook Ads consumption in 2022:

- From Business Manager to Business Suite: The platform now allows you to fully manage your business on Facebook and Instagram from a single location, from publishing to placing advertising to evaluating statistics. It now has a fresh look and a slew of new tools, as well as the ability to control anything from the app.

- With iOS14, Apple alters privacy: With iOS 14, Apple

implemented significant modifications aimed at preserving privacy, which have an influence on technologies such as the Facebook pixel, which we will describe below, and its ability to appropriately track user actions.

-

Goodbye, 20% rule: according to recent reports, Facebook is removing the 20% text restriction on advertising images. The platform still encourages keeping text below this percentage since it performs better, but this upgrade gives advertisers more leeway.

What Determines the Price of Facebook Ads?

While there are other factors at play, there are two surefire ways to determine how much Facebook Ads cost: supply and budget.

The total amount of money you are willing to spend on a single ad or advertising campaign is referred to as your budget.

Furthermore, Facebook Ads provides three budget options:

Daily budget: the amount you are willing to spend on a campaign on a daily basis.

Lifetime budget: the total amount you are willing to spend on the campaign.

Facebook Ads Budget and Duration

Your bid is the amount of money you are willing to pay for an ad location. If you do not select an offer, Facebook will generate one for you based on your budget and campaign duration.

Costs of Facebook Ads: Two Factors to Consider

Before we wrap up this part, there are two crucial considerations to remember when considering the pricing of Facebook Ads.

To begin with, you will only be paying a penny more than your nearest competitor's offer.

This implies that if you put your offer to $2 and your competitors' highest bid is $1.22, you will only pay $1.23 for ad placement.

Second, the costs of advertising on Facebook might vary significantly.

Your cost-per-click could be 1.23 dollars one day and 3.12 dollars the next. So keep that in mind at all times. Always keep an eye on Facebook Ads expenses in order to apply the most cost-effective plan for your ecommerce and your budget.

6 Factors Affecting the Cost of Facebook Ads

As previously said, a number of factors determine the cost of Facebook advertising; here are some of the most essential elements.

1. Your intended audience

Reaching people with a specific demographic and psychographic profile is more expensive. As a result, if you're trying to reach a very desirable audience, your Facebook advertising expenses will be greater.

It is solely a matter of supply and demand. As a result, you may be tempted to limit your target audience in order to narrow your audience, but proceed with caution.

Because there is less space available for advertisements, creating a smaller target audience can result in greater expenditures.

The trick is to discover the appropriate balance, or the balance that works best for your company, and to do so, you must never stop testing and experimenting with different ideas.

2. Your marketing objective

When you create an ad with Facebook Ads, you will be asked to select a marketing goal.

The marketing target you select can have a significant impact on the cost of Facebook advertising.

In general, creating sales is more expensive than simply marketing your brand. In other words, conversions are frequently more expensive than clicks, which are typically more expensive than video views.

Of course, it all relies on your objectives, and you may have various objectives at different times!

3. Your adversaries

This is without a doubt the most important factor impacting

Facebook ad costs. Why? Again, everything comes down to basic economics: supply and demand.

There would be little demand if no other companies were attempting to reach the same target demographic as you, and hence your Facebook Ads expenses would be reduced.

But let's go back to business. Your marketing costs will be heavily influenced by the number of competitors you have, how much they are willing to spend, and their relevance rates.

This is another incentive to keep a watch on your competitors' marketing strategies.

4. When you decide to advertise Competition is higher at peak times. As a result, Facebook advertising expenses are likely to rise in the run-up to Christmas, Black Week, or other holidays.

Furthermore, the day of the week and even the particular periods when you run your Facebook Advertisements will influence the cost of the ads. As a result, the timing of your sponsored posts on social media will affect the cost of your adverts.

5. Your ad's positioning

Your Facebook advertising can be placed in a variety of ways. Here's a quick rundown of the Facebook Ads spots that are still available in 2022:

Facebook

Feed

Articles

In-stream videos

Right column

Marketplace

Stories

Instagram

Messenger

Messages

Sponsored posts

Sites and apps

Banner

Interstitial

Awarded video

Facebook ads have varying pricing based on positioning as well.

Your relevance score

The relevance score is a Facebook metric that assesses your ad's relevance to your target demographic.

The relevance score of your ad rises as users interact with it. However, if a large number of users ignore your ad or click on "this ad is not relevant," your score will fall.

This is very crucial. If your ad has a high relevance score, the Facebook algorithm will favor it and it may even cost less for the same locations.

It is therefore critical to ensure that your sponsored posts are relevant to your target market; otherwise, you will not only waste money on ineffective ads, but you will also be penalized by the platform's algorithm, and your subsequent ads will be more expensive.

8 Ways to Cut the Cost of Facebook Ads

Now that you've learned about the key cost drivers for Facebook Ads, let's look at how you can cut your advertising expenditure on this social network.

While many elements are outside your control, these eight tactics will undoubtedly help you achieve a higher return on investment (ROI).

1. A/B testing

A/B testing is the process of running the same ad campaign twice with a minor change to see how it performs.

Consider the following example. Gymshark has two marketing campaigns with identical content but distinct imagery. This signifies that the company is running an A/B test on the photos to discover which one resonates more with its target demographic.

A/B testing allows you to continuously tweak your advertisements for improved performance. This lowers the cost of Facebook advertising, increasing your return on investment.

Too many advertisers establish a Facebook advertising campaign and then abandon it or forget about it. Do not attempt it.

Some businesses have cut their Facebook advertising prices by 96 percent merely by changing the text! In other words, there's no way to know what works best until you try it. On the other hand, each firm and audience has unique requirements.

The good news is that doing A/B tests in Facebook Ads Manager is quite simple. Simply enable "Create A/B test" in the "Traffic" column. Facebook will divide your budget evenly between the two ads and will allow you to track their performance.

Ideally, you should test each component of your ad individually but start with the image and content.

2. Concentrate on one goal at a time.

When you begin developing a Facebook ad, the first step is to select a goal.

Whatever you decide, be sure that every aspect of your advertising plan contributes to your overall purpose.

Attempting to combine two goals into one ad will not result in a higher return. In fact, it is almost probable that it will increase your Facebook Ads prices and have the opposite effect than you anticipated. Why? Each objective serves a particular purpose and necessitates distinct messaging, audience, content, and pictures. You must keep your adverts as focused as possible.

When you focus on one goal at a time, you can ensure that your image, copywriting, audience, and Call to Action are direct and result in conversions. Create more campaigns and adverts if you wish to focus on more than one target.

Eventually, you will notice that this method will assist you in lowering your Facebook Ads prices.

3. Keep a high relevance score.

As previously stated, the relevance score is a Facebook metric that assesses the relevance of your ad to your target demographic.

A high relevance score indicates that your ad is eliciting good responses and achieving optimal levels of engagement, clicks, and conversions. Ads with a high score reduce the cost of Facebook Ads. The key here is to simply design great advertisements that resonate with your target demographic.

4. Keep track of the frequency

Facebook tracks the frequency of each ad, which is how frequently the same user sees your ad.

If the same people see your ad more than once, one of two things happens:

1. You do not reach out to new people.

2. The folks you're contacting are still seeing your

advertising but aren't converting.

The higher your frequency, the lower your interaction, clicks, and conversions. As a result, the cost of your Facebook advertising will rise.

It is true that some consumers will have to see your adverts several times before clicking on them and becoming clients. However, most prospective purchasers only need to see them once or twice.

As a result, attempt to limit your ad frequency to three or fewer. If your attendance score becomes too high, you should pause and edit or cancel the campaign.

5. Keep your advertisements current.

You must regularly update your advertising and develop new ones. It's also a beneficial habit, in addition to helping to keep attendance low. No matter how good your advertising effort is, it will ultimately lose its effectiveness. This does not, however, imply that you must start from scratch every time. You may maintain the same audience while changing your offer, image, or content. In addition, utilize what you've learned from A/B testing for your new advertising initiatives.

Let's take a look at an example from the Quad Lock brand.

6. Determine an audience for each campaign.

Each marketing should have a specific target demographic in mind. In other words, you should not conduct every campaign with your complete target demographic in mind. This will raise the price of Facebook Ads. Why?

Users will be at various stages of the sales funnel, and as a result, they will require various advertising messages. You will be able to build highly targeted communications, offers, and Calls to Action by segmenting your target demographic into parts and subsections.

As a result, Improved ad effectiveness and cheaper ad expenses on Facebook.

Assume you want to execute a campaign to connect with new potential customers. Even showing these adverts to folks who have already liked your Facebook page would be inefficient.

Instead, you may ban these users, and your target demographic will suddenly be far more inclined to interact with your material.

Facebook provides a plethora of audience targeting choices; it is up to you to take advantage of them!

7. Make use of retargeting and remarketing tactics.

Retargeting and remarketing are marketing methods that allow you to advertise to people who have already been exposed to your company.

The process of presenting advertising to potential customers based on their browser cookies is known as retargeting (using the Facebook pixel).

The process of delivering advertising to potential customers based on email interactions is known as remarketing. In other words, if someone has visited your website or subscribed to

118

your mailing list, they will be able to see your Facebook adverts.

These people are already familiar with your brand and products, so the groundwork for creating and keeping a relationship is already in place.

As a result, retargeting usually leads to more clicks and conversions, as well as decreased advertising expenses. Facebook also has a plethora of remarketing options.

You can target those who have liked your Facebook page, followed you on Instagram, or registered to your mailing list, among other things.

Another intriguing aspect is that the creation of these types of campaigns for the sale of products can be partially automated thanks to Facebook Dynamic Ads: with this type of ad, the social network will show the most appropriate product for the potential customer, based on the person's history of interaction with your company.

8. Restrict your offer

This is the most straightforward method for lowering Facebook Ads costs. If you know you don't want to spend more than $1 on each ad, simply establish a maximum bid limit to ensure you don't pay more.

Of course, this means you may be missing out on prospective ad spots.

Setting an upper limit, on the other hand, is the way to go if you have a marketing budget and need to keep Facebook advertising expenditures under control.

A Facebook Ads campaign might range in price, but in most industries, you can anticipate paying between $0.50 and $2.00 per click.

However, the only way to find out how much Facebook advertising will cost you is to test it out for yourself. So, start with some campaigns and work your way up from there.

Keep in mind that there are six major criteria that influence the cost of your Facebook ads:

1. The intended audience

2. Marketing objective

3. Competitor

4. In advertising

5. Advertisement placement

6. the relevance score

To cut the cost of Facebook advertising, you can:

Do A/B tests

Focus on one goal at a time

Keep relevance scores high

Keep attendance scores low

Update your ads

Select a specific audience for each campaign

Use retargeting and remarketing

Limit your offer

CHAPTER 11

SOCIAL MEDIA MARKETING

No firm, whether B2B or B2C, can neglect Social Media Marketing because that is where customers spend their time and obtain information. Here's how to create an effective strategy: channel selection, material to be posted, the most common management systems, campaign performance indicators, and ROI calculation.

The habit of consulting and posting on social networks is becoming more ingrained, particularly among younger generations, and this is why Social Media Marketing (and thus the Social Media Manager) is gaining a more strategic function in the firm. According to the, We Are Social "Digital 2020" report, social media users worldwide surpassed 3.8 billion (+ 9.2 percent) in January, out of a population of 7.7 billion.

What Is Social Media Marketing (SMM) in 2020, and Why Do We Need It?

To begin, we must define Social Media Marketing. SMM is a type of digital marketing that promotes a company's products and services through social networks and networking platforms. The goal is to be located where the client spends the majority of his time, producing a visibility on online communities and social networks through integrated and organic communication and marketing management across all platforms.

The purpose of Social Network Marketing is to generate interactions with consumers and prospects by focusing on shared values and interests, in order to create affinity with the message recipient and make him attached to the brand. Communications and marketing efforts - it is also possible to sell through social platforms - are bidirectional and thus very engaging. It is possible to build direct discussions with consumers and prospects via social media, as well as receive real-time feedback on products or digital advertising campaigns. Investing in Social Media Marketing enables the company to increase brand awareness, reply to inquiries about the offer, quickly promote new products and services, and direct purchasing decisions while working with a restricted budget.

Business email enables the sending of promotional communications relating to third-party products and services to Joint Controllers in the manufacturing, services (particularly ICT), and trade sectors, using automated and traditional contact methods by the third parties themselves, to whom the data is communicated.

Platforms for Social Networking That Are Available

Let's take a look at the platforms that marketers are most likely to use for their Social Media Marketing initiatives.

Facebook

Average monthly users: 2.44 billion

Target: 18-45 + years

Industries (B2B and B2C): e-commerce, fashion, retail,

banking, financial services, insurance, entertainment, real estate, healthcare

A company cannot avoid having a presence on Facebook, whether it works in B2B or B2C. This platform combines the greatest elements of practically all social media platforms and provides the brand with a concrete way to meet its target audience. Facebook might be used by the company to share content, engage consumers, provide assistance, and display adverts.

Twitter

The average number of monthly users is 340 million. Age range: 18-45+ years

Average monthly users: 340 million

Target: 18-45 + years

Industries (B2B and B2C): news, tech, e-commerce, retail,

travel, sport, healthcare, telco

Twitter is primarily used by brands for customer service because it is the channel that customers prefer for quick interactions with the brand. Twitter users are the most habituated to digital technologies, and the platform has evolved into a resource for learning about businesses, goods, and events.

LinkedIn

Average monthly users: 303 million

Target: 25-45 years

Industries (mainly B2B): legal, tech, manufacturing, marketing, HR, education

Being visible on LinkedIn is required for a B2B corporation because this media provides multiple options for the brand's business to flourish. B2C brands mostly utilize LinkedIn to find potential employees, with little use of the platform for marketing-related promotional activities.

Instagram

Average monthly users: 1 billion

Target: 18-35 years

Industries (mainly B2C): e-commerce, retail, fashion, food & beverage, beauty, entertainment, travel, real estate

Instagram is a mobile platform that emphasizes the visual component of engagement by allowing users to share videos and photographs.

Its popularity has grown exponentially in recent years, and the trend does not appear to be slowing down because it caters to consumers' preferences for vertical videos, live shows, and stories - formats with a high visual impact, usable in a simple manner, and with a very short duration, rarely exceeding a minute.

Those who offer tangible things with a strong design component cannot help but enable Instagram shopping, a feature that many experts predict will be the future of social commerce.

YouTube

Average monthly users: 2 billion

Target: 18-55 + years

Industries (B2B and B2C): Virtually any industry and brand can create effective video content for marketing purposes

YouTube is a video-sharing website that allows users, including individuals and businesses, to view, share, and publish video material. Because of the exponential rise of video marketing, firms are increasing their use of this social network to increase engagement. Consider that YouTube is the world's second most popular search engine, trailing only Google.

Pinterest

Average monthly users: 322 million

Target: 18-45 years

Industries (mainly B2C): photography, art, beauty, ecommerce, fashion, architecture, food, DIY

Pinterest is a visual website that provides a wealth of inspiration for artists and crafters. There are a plethora of ideas in the shape of photographs and cards on a variety of topics, and businesses dealing with DIY, fashion, and catering will find the ideal audience for their marketing campaigns here.

Snapchat

Average monthly users: 382 million

Target: 18-35 years

Industries (mainly B2C): retail, health, food & beverage, event management, fashion

Snapchat is another mobile visual platform that has grown in popularity due to its content's short-term visibility. Snapchat pictures and videos are deleted after 24 hours. It is still a popular medium among Millennials and Generation Z, and marketers mostly utilize it to distribute advertising messages directed at these demographics.

TikTok

It is also worth mentioning TikTok, a social network mostly used by very young people that are making inroads into the marketing tactics of some firms that target this demographic.

Setting Up a Social Media Marketing Campaign

For each target demographic and objective, there are different platforms that can be employed for a Social Media Marketing campaign. As a result, it is critical to properly organize the actions to be carried out in order to maximize the potential of each media and achieve marketing and sales objectives by allocating the budget in the most effective manner. Let's try to condense all we need to do into a few bullet points.

Carry out an audit

It is important to learn what has worked in the past before defining goals and developing a social marketing strategy. A smart place to start is to go to the analytics and insights area of each account and jot down all of the demographic data of the audience as well as what type of content has worked well. Even referral traffic research (from links on other websites that go to the firm's website) can be beneficial in determining which social networks channel the most traffic. Evaluating rivals' behavior is unquestionably a good thing to undertake.

Establish objectives and metrics.

Whether it is to increase brand awareness, engage, generate leads, or increase reach (thus raising interest in posts and tweets), the objectives of a Social Media Marketing strategy must be extremely clear from the start. These must be linked with measurements and KPIs that allow you to see the campaign's development at a glance, as well as which goals have been accomplished and which have not.

If the goal is to increase the brand's visibility on social media, the metrics that will be prioritized are reach (how many people saw the post) and impressions.

If, on the other hand, the firm's goal is to increase traffic from social networks, the Click Through Rate (CTR) will be prioritized, which indicates how many readers who were interested in a post clicked on the link included within and visited the company website.

Finally, if the goal is to convert, i.e., to persuade the target of the article to take an action such as subscribing to a newsletter, installing an App, or purchasing, the Bounce Rate is an important measure to examine. It reveals how soon a person who visited the website abandoned it.

Investigate the intended audience.

The preceding point's audit already provides some information about the company's social audience. The last stage is to create audience personas, which represent the typical characteristics of the target audience - demographics, content preferences, jobs, and interests.

Create a content strategy.

The social content management strategy must be formed by the established objectives as well as the audience personas that have been recognized as relevant.

The audience must be intrigued, informed, engaged, and persuaded by the topic. The definition of an editorial calendar will allow you to automate the process of publishing pieces using one of the numerous platforms accessible.

Create a premium strategy (if any)

Paid social media advertisements help you to increase traffic to your institution's website, improve brand awareness and engagement, and generate more leads and sales.

Track, measure and optimize

Social media marketing is a never-ending activity with a significant experimental component. We're talking about Social Media Management, and there are a lot of tools to aid with that.

As a result, we must not be overwhelmed by any unfavorable or inconsistent results, but rather recognize that SMM is a continuous process of tweaking and adjusting. What was enjoyable last month may no longer be so today.

New social networks develop user confidence, and it may be advantageous to integrate them into the campaign. Followers are typically enthralled by new trends, so stay up to date on fashion trends and, if required, make them your own.

Define your objectives.

Setting specific targets is the first stage in developing a well-thought-out SMM strategy. You can begin with simple aims such as boosting the visibility of content (number of likes or shares), or you can begin with more complicated targets such as increasing website traffic, improving opinions expressed (comments), and creating new leads/customers.

By comparing our activities to those of our competitors, we will be able to determine where to discover a potential audience and which networks are favored by our target audience.

It is quite possible that a corporation has already activated one (or more) social accounts, therefore we must begin with those to determine which ones should be kept active and which should be closed.

The profiles that are still active will be improved in order to drive more organic traffic (from search engines) to the corporate website. They will, however, be promoted on other social networks in order to expand the reach of the posted information.

Make an editing plan.

Quality. This is the crucial word for social media success. Marketers should consequently have a solid Social Media Marketing strategy in place. The document must include all of the SMM strategies' objectives, actions to be performed, target personas, accounts to be used to achieve the goal, the various forms of material offered, and the calendar of associated releases.

The plan must specify who will be responsible for creating the contents, the dates and times of publication of the messages (posts and tweets), and the tone of voice to be used - taking into account, for example, that an easy and spontaneous language should be reserved above all for customer engagement, whereas a less informal language is preferable when promoting the brand's image and values or managing customer service.

If you don't have a clear notion, the so-called "Rule of Thirds" is an excellent beginning point for knowing how to build your editorial plan for your Social Media Marketing campaigns.

1/3 of the contents disseminated on social networks must promote the company's business, its culture, and its values, to convert surfers into prospects.

1/3 of the contents disseminated on social networks must promote ideas and stories concerning the sector to which they belong.

1/3 of the contents disseminated on social networks must promote the brand or products by leveraging 1: 1 interaction to convert and generate profits.

Choose the management platforms.

The management of social accounts is frequently given to a Social Media Manager, even if in certain firms, this activity falls under the purview of the marketing department. This might be a time-consuming operation as well. This is especially true with the Social Media Marketing plans' imposed progressive increase of content publication.

Every day, companies receive thousands of remarks and questions, and even the largest social staff cannot respond to these requests immediately.

However, there is a plethora of software available that allows you to post, monitor, and manage all of your company's social profiles from a single interface, automating the majority of the tasks.

Here is a (non-exhaustive) list of the most popular Social Media Management tools:

• **Buffer**. Buffer is the most widely used dashboard for centrally creating and managing social campaigns on Facebook, Twitter, Instagram, LinkedIn, and Pinterest, as well as for measuring the performance of uploaded content in real-time.

• **Hootsuite**. This is a program that allows you to schedule posts across around twenty different Social Media Marketing sites. It includes capabilities for scheduling, curating, and increasing the effectiveness of submitted information by focusing on the ideal time to publish. Furthermore, it keeps track of all mentions and other audience involvement actions. Facebook, Twitter, Instagram, LinkedIn, YouTube, and Pinterest are all supported.

Sprout Social. This platform includes all of the most helpful features for scheduling posts, monitoring competitor activity, and tracking all keywords. The Smart Inbox tool enables Social Media Managers and specialists to respond to all messages received from numerous social networks from a single interface.

Mentioned in social media. It is a tool for monitoring and tracking all social media activity. It notifies you of everyone who discusses the brand, company, or themes that have been designated as significant for a certain SMM campaign. It collects all user-generated content from various social networks, which can then be readily examined, and it provides a highly valuable influencer rating tool.

- **SEMrush**. This suite monitors all company social profiles and compares their performance to the competition's, determining the best performing content and tracing all social audience interactions.

Resurrect an old post. It is a program that allows you to re-share previously posted content. Its plugin lets you specify the time gap between the two posts (the original and the resumption) as well as the number of posts you want to reshare. The free version only supports Facebook and Twitter, but the premium version allows you to re-share posts from additional platforms such as Pinterest or LinkedIn.

- **Snaplytics**. This is a program created exclusively for managing Snapchat activities, the app that allows users to create and manage very brief stories (on average 20 snaps, about 2 minutes). Analytics allows you to organize tales using tags. It provides insights and information on the progress of the stories, as well as a database of all previous content published in order to learn how they functioned and, if necessary, republish them. It also offers the functionality of postponed publishing.

- **Brandwatch**. It's a social listening application that scours forums, news sites, blogs, and social networks for interesting data to help with social sentiment analysis. As a result, we can determine whether the brand and company are held in high regard and trust by web users. Hubspot Social Media. The Hubspot marketing automation platform includes this Social

134

Media Management software. Its key advantages are the potential to simplify social network management by prioritizing connections between platforms and monitoring engagement and mentions on the major networks.

Zoho Social It provides a simple but effective user interface for managing the brand's social media activity and allows you to track the progress of conversations and brand citations on desired keywords in real-time.

• **Tweetdeck**. It has evolved into an essential management tool for corporate Twitter accounts. From a single console, you can filter follower communications and watch all activity on hashtags, tweets, messages, notifications, and trend topics.

• **StatusBrew**. It is a Social Media Management software intended for cross-functional use by sales, marketing, and customer service departments. It allows you to automatically manage Social Media Marketing campaigns and track all engagement activities, as well as integrate with marketing platforms and social collaboration tools like Mailchimp and Slack.

• Facebook Page Manager is a program that allows you to manage your Facebook page. It is a smartphone app that allows you to manage your Facebook and Instagram accounts while on the go.

2022 ideas, tips, and best practices

The first step in any Social Media Marketing strategy is to build a digital presence on the networking platforms that best reflect the company's image and offer. The second phase is to work on brand awareness, hence raising brand awareness.

The company's goal at a higher level of sophistication will be to be able to better engage prospects and customers through a targeted content management strategy and then divert traffic to the website.

Marketers utilize social media to highlight popular networking platforms, identify and reach consumers and prospects, promote products and services, and engage audiences in order to boost marketing campaign conversion and ROI.

Each platform has its own set of precise standards that describe the measures that must be taken to maximize communication efficacy.

The photo's resolution and picture, for example, the use of hashtags or shortened links, and the date and time of publication. Knowledge of these best practices is a concern for the Social Media Manager, an increasingly significant individual within firms who is in charge of creating a rich and engaging social media experience for each follower.

To maintain basic consistency in the messages transmitted via social media, it is best practice to disseminate a manual outlining the communication policies to be followed when referencing the company or its brands, particularly in terms of the type of content disseminated and tone of voice. To maximize content development, consider significant subjects to the company that is marked with a specific temporal frequency - weekly, monthly, seasonal - or ride current trend issues. This will increase engagement and the effectiveness of Social Media Marketing initiatives.

Investing in influencers will require careful consideration.

These web icons have a lot of likes, and as true brand advocates, they may persuade thousands (often millions) of followers to buy one or the other brand. Influencers are particularly efficient at attracting usually more difficult audiences to paid advertising, serving as authoritative guarantors of the offer's quality.

Make a piece of content go viral while also paying attention to the customer.

Social media marketing efforts have a far greater conversion rate than traditional marketing campaigns. Each encounter with the client helps you to increase his trust, as well as the trust of the communities in which he participates, by activating the "word of mouth" processes that aid in conversion goals. If a company is successful in publishing fascinating material, followers will be accessible to offer it to family and friends, spreading it and therefore increasing the pool of possible prospects.

The password is causing the material to go viral, which is a difficult goal to attain but one that all Social Media Marketing campaigns should strive for.

Brands that are successful on social media share customer posts - unboxing, in-store purchase, guidance - and solicit their feedback. In this approach, the company shows its followers that it cares about them and appreciates their decision to publicly support the brand.

Constantly post

Social networks are a vital source of accurate consumer data, as well as a store of information that is available at any time.

Users use social media to learn, have fun, share ideas, and seek guidance. As a result, it is critical for the organization to maintain constant communication with its target audience.

Otherwise, consumers may wind up appreciating and spreading the competitor's material rather than ours.

The most effective SMM tactics show the company is ready to give advice on how to choose the product as well as how to best use it.

Sharing the articles of bloggers that deal with important themes for the firm allows you to capture the public's attention and provides intriguing ideas for updating. But there must also be room for entertainment, such as memes, quizzes, and hilarious videos.

The Benefits of Social Media Marketing for Businesses

The major advantages of Social Media Marketing are the personalization of communication methods and the precise knowledge of one's target.

The ability to feel the pulse of those who interact with the brand in real-time by tracking shares, likes, posts and reposts, tweets, and retweets enables marketers to maximize campaign success.

The social team's job is not an exercise in style, but rather a series of data-driven actions led by the outcomes acquired for each campaign or even each individual message or post.

Social Media Marketing provides potentially tremendous benefits to the brand for very small investments when compared to traditional promotion and advertising methods. But what are the primary benefits of the SMM? The following are the five most obvious:

1. Establishing itself in the buried memory of the customer

Online communities are drowning in a flood of information. In this regard, psychologists refer to FOMO (fear of missing out), or individuals' dread of being virtually excluded from potentially crucial social events and circumstances. In the midst of all of this, brands are constantly looking for new ways to stand out, and the proverb "out of sight, out of mind" fits nicely into the position of the modern consumer, who is bombarded with a plethora of stimuli and flattery. Companies may use social media to post material on a frequent basis, allowing them to stay one step ahead of the consumer. Even if this does not result in immediate action, such as a purchase or download, the memory will return at the appropriate time.

2. Make the offer more relevant to the consumer's demands. The study of social network interactions and dialogues enables the company to better understand the needs of each individual consumer, as well as the strengths and, conversely, the gaps in the offer. This will enable product, service, and communication innovations to be designed in response to market demand.

3. Obtain new ideas and content

Marketers can benefit from an abundance of information. Indeed, with the help of social networks, the company has access to a plethora of ideas and innovations, which manifest as news, updates, content posted by competitors, and suggestions and criticisms published by customers. Today's brands are built on newsjacking strategies (the art of knowing how to exploit the clamor of the day's news to attract interest in one's offer, the brand, or the company's activities) and popular reviews of the editorial contents used to boost the effectiveness of Social Media Marketing strategies. Crowdsourcing, as represented by so-called user-generated materials, is another method for developing an editorial offer that meets the needs of the social audience.

4. Handle reputation issues and emergencies

Customers comment about the firm and its products whether or not the brand is active on social media. This implies they will continue to make suggestions, requests, and complaints. The ability of the brand to use social media proactively might show to be an effective approach in terms of engagement as well as improving customer service. As a result, social media proves to be vital for managing the most critical business issues in real-time.

5. Increase the effectiveness of advertising

Unlike traditional ADV campaigns, social media advertising is still highly effective. Social networking platforms enable the organization to function in a highly targeted manner. The in-depth understanding of consumer likes, habits, and experiences gathered through social profile analysis enables the delivery of "surgical" and individualized advertising. Remarketing functions on social networks enable you to reawaken the attention of clients who have been inactive for a while. The transfer of comparable audiences, on the other hand, allows the organization to discover new segments of prospects on social networks who share qualities and tastes similar to those of existing consumers.

Produce revenue

Today, social media is a critical touchpoint for guiding leads through the funnel. Social commerce, or the direct sale of products and services via social networks, is a marketing strategy that is becoming more popular in our country. Consumers can explore and compare product offerings on Facebook, Twitter, or Pinterest (all of which have already enabled this feature), and then complete the purchase within the same network.

Is it possible to calculate the return on investment of social media marketing?

By definition, social marketing is data-driven marketing. The ability to conduct A/B tests to analyze the efficacy of each message, article, or post helps you to work more precisely to make the contents align with the desires of the target audience. However, this is frequently insufficient to determine whether the activities performed have ensured the anticipated return on investment.

Measuring the ROI and sales effectiveness of social advertising remains difficult because engagement on these networks does not always transfer into a rise in turnover, at least in the short term. The first goal of a firm that tackles Social Media Marketing can thus be to boost the brand's reputation and online presence, i.e., brand awareness, loyalty, lead generation, or customer experience. And in this scenario, the ROI is difficult to calculate, even if the majority of these objectives are easily observable through the number of shares, likes, tweets, retweets, and mentions.

The Social Media Analytics tools, particularly Google Analytics, are critical for the work of the Social Media Manager and the marketing team, providing a foundation for estimating the ROI of social media marketing initiatives.

Individuals' habits on the corporate website are accurately tracked by the platform. And if this occurs quickly after a post or a tweet, it is easy to conclude that the two behaviors are a result of one another.

Furthermore, the Google platform has a very crucial tool called "Social Conversions," which helps to determine which networks performed better inside a social campaign.

The sales objectives are simply measurable in terms of increased turnover, but the conversion objectives can also be economically evaluated. How? Multiplying the client's average customer lifetime value (which can be found on various websites) by the conversion rate (for example, the number of people who received an e-mail message and clicked on the link contained therein). This allows for a more precise estimation of the potential value of a website visit.

If that isn't enough, apps like Hootsuite, Tweetdeck, and Mention monitor sentiment (i.e., the attitude to evaluate the brand favorably or badly) and the tone of social media dialogues.

CHAPTER 12

10 FACEBOOK TRENDS YOU NEED TO KNOW FOR 2022

Facebook is one of the most popular advertising platforms (if not the most important of all). Keeping up with all of the news is the only way to fully utilize it.

So, what will the Facebook trends be in 2022? You've come to the right place if you're looking for an answer to these questions. We've produced a list of the top Facebook trends for 2022 in this chapter.

1. The Ascension of Facebook Live

The emergence of Facebook Live is undoubtedly one of the most intriguing Facebook trends for 2021.

As we all know, the year 2020 was defined by the epidemic and the lockdown enforced by governments around the world: as a result, many have resorted to using Facebook Live to obtain that small dosage of human contact, although virtual.

According to the most recent data, Facebook Live usage climbed by 26.9 percent in 2019 compared to the previous year. It is worth noting that this increase began in the second quarter of 2020, indicating that the change did not occur due to simple seasonal factors, but for far deeper reasons.

In Q2 2020, the number of Facebook Live postings accounted for roughly 1% of all branded posts on Facebook. This implies that businesses are beginning to recognize the advantages of using Facebook Live to communicate with their clients. Given all of this, it is reasonable to anticipate a growth in the popularity and effectiveness of live broadcasts during 2021.

2. Everyone Is Obsessed With Augmented Reality

The market for Augmented Reality (AR) and Virtual Reality (VR) is quickly expanding, with a projected value of 18.8 billion dollars in 2020. As a result, augmented reality has all the credentials to alter Facebook and become a fad in 2021 (and beyond!).

In this regard, Facebook's Spark AR study is extremely popular among its users. To date, it has been utilized by approximately 500,000 developers from 190 countries to create and post over 1.2 million AR effects on Facebook and Instagram.

But wait, there's more! According to statistics, consumers have really grown into it in the last few months. AR effects provided by over 150 accounts alone received over a billion views in the third quarter of 2020.

Given the rapid adoption of AR by consumers and its rapid development in popularity, we can confidently predict that we are witnessing one of the hottest Facebook trends of 2021.

3. Video Marketing Is Increasing

You are probably aware that videos are the most popular type of material among consumers, particularly on social media.

The most current Facebook trends reveal a definite growth in the number of videos submitted on the platform. Overall, the proportion climbed by 2.6 percent in the third quarter of 2020 as compared to the same period last year.

In fact, behind photographs (which account for 70% of all Facebook content), videos have surpassed images as the second most popular post type on the platform. They currently account for 17% of all posted content, including pressing links and status updates.

If video marketing is one of the Facebook trends you're considering, bear in mind that the most effective films range in length from 65 seconds to 5 minutes.

4. People adore Facebook groups.

Passions and interests have the capacity to link and unite people from all over the world with vastly diverse histories and cultural origins.

Facebook groups are a prime example of this behavior. Every month, more than 1.4 billion people join over 10 million Facebook groups.

Based on this information, you may, on the one hand, start your own group to connect with clients and, on the other hand, join several Facebook groups to uncover new opportunities for trade and comparison and to grow your brand.

What are the benefits of using Facebook groups? What is the source of their popularity? It is most likely owing to the moderate setting, which provides a light social experience. The communities that form are guided by love and assistance, which is exactly what people appreciate.

A good trend that is likely to continue till 2022. Are you prepared to join us in riding this tidal wave?

5. Facebook Shop: It's Time to Go Online Shopping

Consumers will increasingly shop online. Is it surprising to you?

Most likely not.

For many years, online shopping has been an important part of their life. The pandemic, the progressive collapse of local businesses, and the ecommerce boom have all radically affected consumption habits and opened the floodgates of internet commerce to numerous firms (especially small and medium-sized ones).

Faced with this upheaval, Facebook has been anything but inactive! It will launch its Facebook Shop in 2020.

"We're introducing Facebook Shops and investing in features in our applications that encourage people to shop and make online buying and selling easier."

Facebook Shop enables any business owners to start their own online store on the network with the goal of marketing and selling their products.

As online buying becomes the standard rather than the exception, it is projected that more and more businesses will use Facebook Shop as an extra sales channel. Why is there so much interest in Facebook shopping? Obviously, because of the enormous popularity of this social network and its 2.6 billion users.

6. Facebook's News Section Is the Queen of the Ads

Because Facebook is one of the most essential and widely utilized social media platforms in digital marketing, it is critical to stay current on its developments. But beware: we're not only talking about consuming habits and user behavior here; we're also talking about advertising strategies.

According to the most recent data, Facebook's news feed received 58.2 percent of firms' ad expenditure in the third quarter of 2020, beating in-stream video and video.

When comparing the three placements, advertising in Facebook's news section had a substantially higher overall CTR (Click Through Rate) than in-stream videos and videos - 1.82 percent versus 0.85 percent and 0.65 percent, respectively.

It's no surprise, then, that businesses choose to concentrate their social media advertising efforts on Facebook's news feed.

7. The Use of Chatbots Is Growing

Consumers today expect things to be quick and easy, and this includes not only product delivery but also communication with businesses.

And it is in this framework that we can best comprehend the enormous popularity of chatbots on Facebook Messenger. Growth is expected to increase from 2.6 billion dollars in 2019 to 9.4 billion dollars by 2024.

As a result, it is projected that more and more businesses will choose to use a chatbot by the end of 2022. These will join the 40 million brands that have already opted to be present on Facebook Messenger.

Did you know that Facebook Messenger sends over 20 billion messages per month? Truly remarkable! A successful outcome that does not happen by chance: Facebook is continually working to improve the Messenger experience for all users, whether they are individuals or businesses. Among the most recent additions are a calendar for arranging appointments directly through the platform and lead creation tools.

With so many advantages, employing chatbots and Facebook Messenger for business and sales will most definitely be one of the top Facebook trends in 2022.

8. Increased Assistance for Small and Medium-Sized Enterprises

The epidemic has dealt significant economic damage to small and medium-sized enterprises.

According to a recent poll, roughly one-third of SMEs identified access to finance to support cash flow as one of the most significant issues.

Facebook has announced a financial support scheme in an effort to assist the most vulnerable businesses. There is talk of a $100 million grant for 30,000 businesses around the world.

As analysts anticipate that the pandemic will persist until 2022, we may expect Facebook to step up once more to provide additional assistance in some form or another to encourage businesses to promote in order to develop their business.

9. User-Generated Content (UGC)

User-Generated Content (UGC) has long been regarded as one of the most effective and widely used kinds of content marketing.

The closing of recording studios in 2020, on the other hand, has increasingly pushed businesses to seek alternatives to huge productions, resulting in a surge in UGC in terms of both demand and production.

What occurred on Facebook? According to the most recent research, user-generated video material has increased dramatically from 223 billion views in January 2020 to 495 billion in August 2020. The figure has more than doubled in seven months.

Given the benefits of User Generated Content and the continued constraints, this trend is projected to remain favorable and rising. It's impossible not to include user-generated content (UGC) in your list of Facebook trends for 2022.

10. Hashtag Retaliation on Facebook

Hashtags, which were introduced by Twitter more than 10 years ago, have now invaded all social media platforms, from LinkedIn to TikTok, via Facebook, of course! However, Facebook did not stop there. It is now aiming to improve its hashtag feature to help users maximize the reach and engagement of their content.

It is about deploying a feature that will utilize artificial intelligence to propose hashtags to users. Just like on Instagram, this list of key phrases will include the number of posts that use the same hashtag.

All of Zuckerberg's involvement can only imply one thing: hashtags will most likely be one of the hottest Facebook trends in 2022.

Many lament Facebook's quick fall; the truth is that the dependable Mark's social network continues to reign supreme, and his dominance appears set to remain for a long time. Is it still worthwhile to consider it as part of your marketing and advertising strategies? Without a doubt. We hope that our Facebook trends list will advise and help you as you plan for a prosperous and growing 2022.

CHAPTER 13

5 NEWS YOU MISSED

How much news do we publish each day? And how many do we recall? We have a lot of feeds to check between LinkedIn, Facebook, Instagram, and now TikTok, and sometimes some news slips between the cracks.

1) Facebook Messenger and Best Practices for Communicating With Your Desired Buyer

Messenger is being tested at home. Facebook Messenger will plan minor UX experiments in the next weeks with the goal of improving the user experience and making messaging between people and businesses more fluid and engaging.

What is the end goal? Connecting individuals and businesses in a more pleasant and efficient manner.

Here are five best practices for communicating with your audience on Facebook Messenger that is directly advised by Facebook Messenger:

1. Respond swiftly and get your consumer accustomed to receiving prompt and timely responses whenever you are called.

2. Be succinct and courteous. Respond by communicating only the main points and getting right to the point; save your rants for private conversations.

3. Use every Messenger feature available to you: tag users to include them in specific clusters, use appointment reminders, and leverage the potential of Messenger Ads to stay anchored in the mind of your ideal customer and be able to reach them even outside the 24-hour window in which it is permitted to contact him.

4. Ensure that you offer value in your responses, that you do not contact to sell, and that you do not use a salesy approach all of the time. We've mentioned it countless times on these pages: before asking your prospect for even one dime, fill it with value and concreteness.

5. Segment your audience and engage your clients by asking strategic questions that will enable you to develop true sub-groups (e.g., for a restaurant, lovers of a certain type of product rather than another).

2) Is Facebook aiming to be the market leader in virtual reality?

Facebook gives augmented reality a boost. Recently, Zuckerberg's machine announced the acquisition of "Sanzaru Titles," a video game production business best known for authoring one of the most well-known Oculus Rift games, "Asgard's Wrath."

If the love for VR had already manifested itself with the acquisition of the viewer manufacturer, it now appears that the interest is also turning toward the purchase of real software houses, with the goal of expanding the Facebook family's range of services and developing applications and video games.

Who knows if, in the next 10-20 years, Facebook will be acknowledged as the market leader in virtual reality rather than as a social network? We'll see what happens.

3) Twitter Provides Developers with Access to the Hide Replies Function

Twitter has finally made "Hide Replies" available to its developers. The old 140-character social network is attempting to enable its developers to create solutions that allow their users to hide answers beneath their tweets.

Although we do not yet have an official release date, have you ever felt the need for this feature?

4) TikTok as a Traffic Channel: Are We There Yet?

Great and juicy news from TikTok, the first of which is the new feature sticker, which has been "copied" directly from competitor Instagram. This capability allows each maker and user to "stick" a piece of material (in fact, a sticker) into the movie, which will remain fixed in the position set by the user.

But the most intriguing news is something that marketers have been anticipating for a long time.

The link is in the TikTok profile's bio. As for Instagram, this highly helpful tool appears to be on the way, allowing users to drive traffic to specific URLs and take advantage (even more) of this platform as a traffic conduit. This could lead to even more brands joining the platform; we'll see some nice ones, especially if the TikTok ADS is included in the speech.

5) Creators Can Now Be Found on Smartphones: Facebook Has Launched the "Creators" App

Last week, Facebook began testing Creator Studio, a new mobile app devoted to the world of content creators. Many of you will be familiar with the Desktop counterpart, a portion that assists users in creating, posting, and managing material, as well as tracking the performance of each piece of content.

According to Facebook, the app would offer the same levels of "depth" and will assist all producers even (and finally) on mobile. The software will, of course, be accessible for both iOS and Android. Keep an eye out for the official release date.